Charlotte Barber

HALF HOURS

DER TAG

J. M. Barrie

HALF HOURS

DER TAG

BY

J. M. BARRIE

NEW YORK

CHARLES SCRIBNER'S SONS

1923

CONTENTS

HALF HOURS

HALF HOURS

PANTALOON

THE scene makes-believe to be the private
home of PANTALOON and COLUMBINE, though
whether they ever did have a private home is
uncertain.

In the English version (and with that alone
are we concerning ourselves) these two were
figures in the harlequinade which in Victorian
days gave a finish to pantomime as vital as
a tail to a dog. Now they are vanished from
the boards; or at best they wander through the
canvas streets, in everybody's way, at heart
afraid of their own policeman, really dead,
and waiting, like the faithful old horse, for
some one to push them over. Here at the
theatre is perhaps a scrap of COLUMBINE's
skirt, torn off as she squeezed through the
wings for the last time, or even placed there

3

intentionally by her as a souvenir: COL-
UMBINE *to her public, a kiss hanging on a
nail.*

*They are very illusive. One has to toss
to find out what was their relation to each
other: whether* PANTALOON, *for instance, was*
COLUMBINE'S *father. He was an old, old
urchin of the streets over whom some fairy
wand had been waved, rather carelessly, and
this makes him a child of art; now we must
all be nice to children of art, and the nicest
thing we can do for* PANTALOON *is to bring
the penny down heads and give him a delightful daughter. So* COLUMBINE *was* PANTA-
LOON'S *daughter.*

*It would be cruel to her to make her his wife,
because then she could not have a love-affair.*

*The mother is dead, to give the little home
a touch of pathos.*

We have now proved that PANTALOON *and
his daughter did have a home, and as soon as
we know that, we know more. We know,
for instance, that as half a crown seemed almost*

*a competency to them, their home must have
been in a poor locality and conveniently small.
We know also that the sitting-room and kitchen
combined must have been on the ground floor.
We know it, because in the harlequinade they
were always flying from the policeman or
bashing his helmet, and* PANTALOON *would
have taken ill with a chamber that was not
easily commanded by the policeman on his
beat. Even* COLUMBINE, *we may be sure,
refined as she was and incapable of the pettiest
larceny, liked the homely feeling of dodging
the policeman's eye as she sat at meals.
Lastly, we know that directly opposite the
little home was a sausage-shop, the pleasantest
of all sights to* PANTALOON, *who, next to his
daughter, loved a sausage. It is being almost
too intimate to tell that* COLUMBINE *hated
sausages; she hated them as a literary
hand's daughter might hate manuscripts. But
like a loving child she never told her hate,
and spent great part of her time toasting
sausages to a turn before the fire, and eating*

*her own one bravely when she must, but con-
cealing it in the oddest places when she could.*

*We should now be able to reconstitute
PANTALOON'S parlour. It is agreeably stuffy,
with two windows and a recess between them,
from which one may peep both ways for the
policeman. The furniture is in horse-hair,
no rents showing, because careful COLUMBINE
has covered them with antimacassars. All
the chairs (but not the sofa) are as sound of
limb as they look except one, and COLUMBINE,
who is as light as an air balloon, can sit on
this one even with her feet off the floor. Though
the time is summer there is a fire burning,
so that PANTALOON need never eat his sausages
raw, which he might do inadvertently if COL-
UMBINE did not take them gently from his
hand. There is a cosy round table with a
wax-cloth cover adhering to it like a sticking-
plaster, and this table is set for tea. His-
trionic dignity is given to the room by a large
wicker trunk in which PANTALOON'S treasures
are packed when he travels by rail, and on it*

is a printed intimation that he is one of the brightest wits on earth. COLUMBINE *could be crushed, concertina-like, into half of this trunk, and it may be that she sometimes travels thus to save her ticket. Between the windows hangs a glass case, such as those at inns wherein Piscator preserves his stuffed pike, but this one contains a poker. It is interesting to note that* PANTALOON *is sufficiently catholic in his tastes to spare a favourable eye for other arts than his own. There are various paintings on the walls, all of himself, with the exception of a small one of his wife. These represent him not in humorous act but for all time, as, for instance, leaning on a bracket and reading a book, with one finger laid lightly against his nose.*

So far our work of reconstitution has been easy, but we now come to the teaser. In all these pictures save one (to be referred to in its proper place) PANTALOON *is presented not on the stage but in private life, yet he is garbed and powdered as we know him in the harle-*

*quinade. If they are genuine portraits, there-
fore, they tell us something profoundly odd
about the home life of* PANTALOON; *nothing
less than this, that as he was on the stage, so
he was off it, clothes, powder, and all; he
was not acting a part in the harlequinade,
he was merely being himself. It was undoubtedly this strange discovery that set us
writing a play about him.*

*Of course bitter controversy may come of
this, for not every one will agree that we are
right. It is well known among the* cognos-
centi *that actors in general are not the same
off the stage as on; that they dress for their
parts, speak words written for them which
they do not necessarily believe, and afterwards
wash the whole thing off and then go to clubs
and coolly cross their legs. I accept this to
be so (though I think it a pity), but* PANTALOON
*was never an actor in their sense; he would
have scorned to speak words written for him
by any whippersnapper; what he said and
did before the footlights were the result of*

*mature conviction and represented his philoso-
phy of life. It is the more easy to believe
this of him because we are so anxious to believe it of* COLUMBINE. *Otherwise she could
not wear her pretty skirts in our play, and
that would be unbearable.*

*If this noble and simple consistency was
the mark of* PANTALOON *and* COLUMBINE (*as
we have now proved up to the hilt*), *it must have
distinguished no less the other members of the
harlequinade. There were two others, the*
HARLEQUIN *and the* CLOWN.

*In far-back days, when the world was so
young that pieces of the original egg-shell still
adhered to it, one boy was so desperately
poor that he alone of children could not don
fancy dress on fair days. Presently the other
children were sorry for this drab one, so each
of them clipped a little bit off his own clothing
and gave it to him. These were sewn together
and made into a costume for him, by the jolly
little tailors who in our days have quite gone
out, and that is why* HARLEQUIN *has come down*

to us in patchwork. He was a lovely boy with no brains at all (not that this matters), while the CLOWN *was all brain.*

It has been our whim to make PANTALOON *and* COLUMBINE *our chief figures, but we have had to go for them, as it were, to the kitchen; the true head of the harlequinade was the* CLOWN. *You could not become a clown by taking thought, you had to be born one. It was just a chance. If the* CLOWN *had wished to walk over the others they would have spread themselves on the ground so that he should be able to do it without inconveniencing himself. Any money they had they got from him, and it was usually pennies. If they displeased him he caned them. He had too much power and it brutalised him, as we shall see, but in fairness it should be told that he owed his supremacy entirely to his funniness. The family worshipped funniness, and he was the funniest.*

It is not necessary for our play to reconstitute the homes of HARLEQUIN *and* CLOWN, *but it could be done.* HARLEQUIN, *as a bachelor with no means but with a secret conviction that he was a gentleman, had a sitting-and-bed combined at the top of a house too near Jermyn Street for his purse. He made up by not eating very much, which was good for his figure. He always carried his wand, which had curious magical qualities, for instance it could make him invisible; but in the street he seldom asked this of it, having indeed a friendly desire to be looked at. He had delightful manners and an honest heart. The* CLOWN, *who, of course, had appearances to keep up, knew the value of a good address, and undoubtedly lived in the Cromwell Road. He smoked cigars with bands round them, and his togs were cut in Savile Row.*

CLOWN *and* PANTALOON *were a garrulous pair, but* COLUMBINE *and* HARLEQUIN *never spoke. I don't know whether they were what we call dumb. Perhaps if they had tried to talk with their tongues they could have done so, but they never thought of it. They were*

*such exquisite dancers that they did all their
talking with their legs. There is nothing
that may be said which they could not express
with this leg or that. It is the loveliest of all
languages, and as soft as the fall of snow.*

When the curtain rises we see COLUMBINE
*alone in the little house, very happy and gay,
for she has no notion that her tragic hour is
about to strike. She is dressed precisely as
we may have seen her on the stage. It is the
pink skirt, the white one being usually kept
for Sunday, which is also washing-day; and
we almost wish this had been Sunday, just
to show* COLUMBINE *in white at the tub, washing
the pink without letting a single soap-sud pop
on to the white. She is toasting bread rhyth-
mically by the fire, and hides the toasting-fork
as the policeman passes suspiciously outside.
Presently she is in a whirl of emotion because
she has heard* HARLEQUIN'S *knock. She
rushes to the window and hides (they were
always hiding), she blows kisses, and in her
excitement she is everywhere and nowhere at*

once, like a kitten that leaps at nothing and stops half-way. She has the short quick steps of a bird on a lawn. Long before we have time to describe her movements she has bobbed out of sight beneath the table to await HARLE-QUIN *funnily, for we must never forget that they are a funny family. With a whirl of his wand that is itself a dance,* HARLEQUIN *makes the door fly open. He enters, says the stage direction, but what it means is that somehow he is now in the room. He probably knows that* COLUMBINE *is beneath the table, as she hides so often and there are so few places in the room to hide in, but he searches for her elsewhere, even in a jug, to her extreme mirth, for of course she is peeping at him. He taps the wicker basket with his wand and the lid flies open. Still no* COLUMBINE! *He sits dejectedly on a chair by the table, with one foot toward the spot where we last saw her head. This is irresistible. She kisses the foot. She is out from beneath the table now, and he is pursuing her round the room.* **They** *are as wayward as leaves in a gale. The cunning fellow pretends he does not want her, and now it is she who is pursuing him. There is something entrancing in his hand. It is a ring. It is the engagement-ring at last! She falters, she blushes, but she snatches at the ring. He tantalises her, holding it beyond her reach, but soon she has pulled down his hand and the ring is on her finger. They are dancing ecstatically when* PANTALOON *comes in and has to drop his stick because she leaps into his arms. If she were not so flurried she would see that the aged man has brought excitement with him also.*

PANTALOON. Ah, Fairy! Fond of her dad, is she? Sweetest little daughter ever an old 'un had. (*He sees* HARLEQUIN *and is genial to him, while* HARLEQUIN *pirouettes a How-d' ye-do.*) You here, Boy; welcome, Boy. (*He is about to remove his hat in the ordinary way, but* HARLEQUIN, *to save his prospective father-*

in-law any little trouble, waves his wand and the hat goes to rest on a door-peg. The little service so humbly tendered pleases PANTALOON, *and he surveys* HARLEQUIN *with kindly condescension.*) Thank you, Boy. You are a good fellow, Boy, and an artist too, in your limited way, not here (*tapping his head*), not in a brainy way, but lower down (*thoughtfully, and including* COLUMBINE *in his downward survey*). That's where your personality lies—lower down. (*At the noble word personality* COLUMBINE *thankfully crosses herself, and then indicates that tea is ready.*) Tea, Fairy? I have such glorious news; but I will have a dish of tea first. You will join us, Boy? Sit down. (*They sit down to tea, the lovers exchanging shy, happy glances, but soon* PANTALOON *rises petulantly.*) Fairy, there are no sausages! Tea without a sausage. I am bitterly disappointed. And on a day, too, when I have great news. It's almost more than I can bear.

No sausages! (*He is old and is near weeping, but* COLUMBINE *indicates with her personality that if he does not forgive her she must droop and die, and soon again he is a magnanimous father.*) Yes, yes, my pet, I forgive you. You can't abide sausages; nor can you, Boy. (*They hide their shamed heads.*) It's not your fault. Some are born with the instinct for a sausage, and some have it not. (*More brightly*) Would you like me to be funny now, my dear, or shall we have tea first? (*They prefer to have tea first, and the courteous old man sits down with them.*) But you do think me funny, don't you, Fairy? Neither of you can look at me without laughing, can you? Try, Boy; try, Fairy. (*They try, but fail. He is moved.*) Thank you both, thank you kindly. If the public only knew how anxiously we listen for the laugh they would be less grudging of it. (*Hastily*) Not that I have any cause of complaint. Every

night I get the laugh from my gener-
ous patrons, the public, and always
by legitimate means. When I think
what a favourite I am I cannot keep my
seat. (*He rises proudly.*) I am acknowledged by all in the know to be a funny
old man. (*He moves about exultantly,
looking at the portraits that are to hand
him down to posterity.*) That picture of
me, Boy, was painted to commemorate
my being the second funniest man on
earth. Of course Joey is the funniest,
but I am the second funniest. (*They
have scarcely listened; they have been exchanging delicious glances with face and
foot. But at mention of the* CLOWN *they
shudder a little, and their hands seek each
other for protection.*) This portrait I had
took—done—in honour of your birth, my
love. I call it 'The Old 'Un on First
Hearing that He is a Father.' (*He
chuckles long before another picture which
represents him in the dress of ordinary*

people.) This is me in fancy dress; it is
how I went to a fancy-dress ball. Your
mother, Fairy, was with me, in a long
skirt! Very droll we must have looked,
and very droll we felt. I call to mind
we walked about in this way; the way
the public walks, you know. (*In his
gaiety he imitates the walk of the public,
and roguish* COLUMBINE *imitates them also,
but she loses her balance*.) Yes, try it.
Don't flutter so much. Ah, it won't do,
Fairy. Your natural way of walking's
like a bird bobbing about on a lawn after
worms. Your mother was the same
and when she got low in spirits I just
blew her about the room till she was
lively again. Blow Fairy about, Boy.
(HARLEQUIN *blows her divinely about the
room, against the wall, on to seats and off
them, and for some sad happy moments*
PANTALOON *gazes at her, feeling that his
wife is alive again. They think it is the
auspicious time to tell him of their love, but*

*bashfulness falls upon them. He only sees
that their faces shine.*) Ah, she is happy,
my Fairy, but I have news that will make
her happier! (*Curiously*) Fairy, you
look as if you had something you wanted
to tell me. Have you news too?
(*Tremblingly she extends her hand and
shows him the ring on it. For a moment he
misunderstands.*) A ring! Did *he* give
you that? (*She nods rapturously.*) Oho,
oho, this makes me so happy. I 'll be
funnier than ever, if possible. (*At this
they dance gleefully, but his next words
strike them cold.*) But, the rogue! He
said he wanted me to speak to you about
it first. That was my news. Oh, the
rogue! (*They are scared, and sudden
fear grips him.*) There 's nothing wrong,
is there? It was Joey gave you that
ring, wasn't it, Fairy? (*She shakes her
head, and the movement shakes tears from
her eyes.*) If it wasn't Joey, who was it?
(HARLEQUIN *steps forward.*) You! You

are not fond of Boy, are you, Fairy?
(*She is clinging to her lover now, and*
PANTALOON *is a little dazed.*) But, my
girl, Joey wants you. A clown wants
you. When a clown wants you, you are
not going to fling yourself away on a
harlequin, are you? (*They go on their
knees to him, and he is touched, but also
frightened.*) Don't try to get round me;
now don't. Joey would be angry with
me. He can be hard when he likes, Joey
can. (*In a whisper*) Perhaps he would
cane me! You wouldn't like to see your
dad caned, Fairy. (COLUMBINE'S *head
sinks to the floor in woe, and* HARLEQUIN
eagerly waves his wand.) Ah, Boy, you
couldn't defy him. He is our head.
You can do wonderful things with that
wand, but you can't fight Joey with it.
(*Sadly enough the wand is lowered.*) You
see, children, it won't do. You have no
money, Boy, except the coppers Joey
sometimes gives you in an envelope of a

Friday night, and we can't marry without money (*with an attempt at joviality*), can't marry without money, Boy. (Harlequin *with a rising chest produces money*.) Seven shillings and tenpence! You have been saving up, Boy. Well done! But it's not enough. (Columbine *darts to the mantelshelf for her money-box and rattles it triumphantly.* Pantaloon *looks inside it.*) A half-crown and two sixpences! It won't do, children. I had a pound and a piano-case when I married, and yet I was pinched. (*They sit on the floor with their fingers to their eyes, and with difficulty he restrains an impulse to sit beside them.*) Poor souls! poor true love! (*The thought of Joey's power and greatness overwhelms him.*) Think of Joey's individuality, Fairy. He banks his money, my love. If you saw the boldness of Joey in the bank when he hands the slip across the counter and counts his money, my pet, instead of being thankful for what-

ever they give him.   And then he puts out
his tongue at them! The artist in him
makes him put out his tongue at them.
For he is a great artist, Joey. He is a
greater artist than I am. I know it and
I admit it. He has a touch that is
beyond me. (*Imploringly*) Did you say
you would marry him, my love? (*She does
not raise her head, and he continues with a
new break in his voice.*) It is not his
caning me I am so afraid of, but—but
I'm oldish now, Fairy, even for an old
'un, and there is something I must tell
you. I have tried to keep it from myself, but I know. It is this: I am afraid,
my sweet, I am not so funny as I used to
be. (*She encircles his knees in dissent.*)
Yes, it's true, and Joey knows it. On
Monday I had to fall into the barrel three
times before I got the laugh. Joey saw!
If Joey were to dismiss me I could never
get another shop. I would be like a dog
without a master. He has been my

master so long. I have put by nearly
enough to keep me, but oh, Fairy, the
awfulness of not being famous any longer.
Living on without seeing my kind friends
in front. To think of my just being
one of the public, of my being pointed at
in the streets as the old 'un that was
fired out of the company because he
missed his laughs. And that's what
Joey will bring to pass if you don't marry
him, my girl. (*It is an appeal for mercy,
and* COLUMBINE *is his loving daughter.
Her face is wan, but she tries to smile. She
hugs the ring to her breast, and then gives
it back to* HARLEQUIN. *They try to dance
a last embrace, but their legs are leaden.
He kisses her cheeks and her foot and goes
away broken-hearted. The brave girl puts
her arm round her father's neck and hides
her wet face. He could not look at it
though it were exposed, for he has more to
tell.*) I haven't told you the worst yet,
my love. I didn't dare tell you the worst

till Boy had gone. Fairy, the marriage
is to be to-day! Joey has arranged it
all. It's his humour, and we dare not
thwart him. He is coming here to take
you to the wedding. (*In a tremble she
draws away from him.*) I haven't been
a bad father to you, have I, my girl?
When we were waiting for you before
you were born, your mother and I, we
used to wonder what you would be like,
and I—it was natural, for I was always
an ambitious man—I hoped you would
be a clown. But that wasn't to be, and
when the doctor came to me—I was walking up and down this room in a tremble,
for my darling was always delicate—when
the doctor came to me and said, 'I congratulate you, sir, on being the father
of a fine little columbine,' I never uttered
one word of reproach to him or to you
or to her. (*There is a certain grandeur
about the old man as he calls attention to
the nobility of his conduct, but it falls from*

him on the approach of the Clown. *We
hear Joey before we see him: he is singing
a snatch of one of his triumphant ditties,
less for his own pleasure perhaps than to
warn the policeman to be on the alert.
He has probably driven to the end of the
street, and then walked. A tremor runs
through* Columbine *at sound of him, but*
Pantaloon *smiles, a foolish, ecstatic
smile. Joey has always been his hero.*)
Be ready to laugh, my girl. Joey will
be angry if he doesn't get the laugh.

(*The* Clown *struts in, as confident of
welcome as if he were the announce-
ment of dinner. He wears his motley
like an order. A silk hat and an
eye-glass indicate his superior social
position. A sausage protruding from
a pocket shows that he can unbend at
times. A masterful man when you
don't applaud enough, he is at present
in uproarious spirits, as if he had
just looked in a mirror. At first he*

affects not to see his host, to PANTA-
LOON'S *great entertainment.*)

CLOWN. Miaw, miaw!

PANTALOON (*bent with merriment*). He is at
his funniest, quite at his funniest!

    (CLOWN *kicks him hard but good-
naturedly, and* PANTALOON *falls to
the ground.*)

CLOWN. Miaw!

PANTALOON (*reverently*). What an artist!

CLOWN (*pretends to see* COLUMBINE *for the
first time in his life. In a masterpiece of
funniness he starts back, like one dazzled
by a naked light*). Oh, Jiminy Crinkles!
Oh, I say, what a beauty!

PANTALOON. There's nobody like him!

CLOWN. It's Fairy. It's my little Fairy.

    (*Strange, but all her admiration for
this man has gone. He represents
nothing to her now but wealth and
social rank. He ogles her, and she
shrinks from him as if he were something nauseous.*)

PANTALOON (*warningly*). Fairy!

CLOWN (*showing sharp teeth*). Hey, what's this, old 'un? Don't she admire me?

PANTALOON. Not admire you, Joey? That's a good 'un. Joey's at his best to-day.

CLOWN. Ain't she ready to come to her wedding?

PANTALOON. She's ready, Joey.

CLOWN (*producing a cane, and lowering*). Have you told her what will happen to you if she ain't ready?

PANTALOON (*backing*). I've told her, Joey (*supplicating*). Get your hat, Fairy.

CLOWN. Why ain't she dancing wi' joy and pride?

PANTALOON. She is, Joey, she is.

(COLUMBINE *attempts to dance with joy and pride, and the* CLOWN *has been so long used to adulation that he is deceived.*)

CLOWN (*amiable again*). Parson's waiting. Oh, what a lark.

PANTALOON (*with a feeling that lark is not*

perhaps the happiest word for the occasion).
Get your things, Fairy.

CLOWN (*riding on a chair*). Give me something first, my lovey-dovey. I shuts my
eyes and opens my mouth, and waits
for what's my doo. (*She knows what he
means, and it is sacrilege to her. But her
father's arms are extended beseechingly.
She gives the now abhorred countenance
a kiss, and runs from the room. The
CLOWN plays with the kiss as if it were a
sausage, a sight abhorrent to HARLEQUIN,
who has stolen in by the window. Fain
would he strike, but though he is wearing
his mask, which is a sign that he is invisible,
he fears to do so. As if conscious of the
unseen presence, the CLOWN's brow darkens.*)
Joey, when I came in I saw Boy hanging
around outside.

PANTALOON (*ill at ease*). Boy? What can
he be wanting?

CLOWN. I know what he is wanting, and
I know what he will get. (*He brandishes*

the cane threateningly. At the same moment the wedding bells begin to peal.)

PANTALOON. Hark!

CLOWN (*with grotesque accompaniment*). My wedding bells. Fairy's wedding bells. There they go again, here we are again, there they go again, here we are again. (COLUMBINE *returns. She has tried to hide the tears on her cheeks behind a muslin veil. There is a melancholy bouquet in her hand. She passionately desires to be like the respectable public on her marriage day. HARLEQUIN raises his mask for a moment that she may see him, and they look long at each other, those two, who are never to have anything lovely to look at again. 'Won't he save her yet?' says her face, but 'I am afraid' says his. Still the bells are jangling.*)

PANTALOON. My girl.

CLOWN. Mine. (*He kisses her, but it is the sausage look that is in his eyes. PANTALOON, bleeding for his girl, raises his staff*

to strike him, but COLUMBINE *will not have
the sacrifice. She gives her arm to the*
CLOWN.) To the wedding. To the
wedding. Old 'un, lead on, and we
will follow thee. Oh, what a lark!

    (*They are going toward the door, but
in this supreme moment love turns
timid Boy into a man. He waves
his mysterious wand over them, so
that all three are suddenly bereft of
movement. They are like frozen
figures. He removes his mask and
smiles at them with a terrible face.
Fondly and leisurely he gathers* COL-
UMBINE *in his arms and carries her
out by the window. The* CLOWN *and*
PANTALOON *remain there, as if struck
in the act of taking a step forward.
The wedding bells are still pealing.*)

*The curtain falls for a moment only.
It rises on the same room several
years later.*

*The same room, as one may say of
a suit of clothes, out of which the
whilom tenant has long departed,
that they are the same man. A
room cold to the touch, dilapidated,
fragments of the ceiling fallen and
left where they fell, wall-paper peel-
ing damply, portraits of* PANTA-
LOON *taken down to sell, unsaleable,
and never rehung. Once such a
clean room that its ghost to-day might
be* COLUMBINE *chasing a speck of
dust, it is now untended. Even the
windows are grimy, which tells a
tale of* PANTALOON'S *final capitula-
tion; while any heart was left him
we may be sure he kept the windows
clean so that the policeman might
spy upon him. Perhaps the policeman has gone from the street, bored,
nothing doing there now.*

*It is evening and winter time, and the
ancient man is moving listlessly*

*about his room, mechanically blowing
life into his hands as if he had forgotten that there is no real reason why
there should be life in them. The
clothes* COLUMBINE *used to brush
with such care are slovenly, the hair
she so often smoothed with all her
love is unkempt. He is smaller, a
man who has shrunk into himself in
shame, not so much shame that he is
uncared for as that he is forgotten.*

*He is sitting forlorn by the fire when
the door opens to admit his first
visitor for years. It is the* CLOWN,
*just sufficiently stouter to look more
resplendent. The drum, so to say, is
larger. He gloats over the bowed*
PANTALOON *like a spiteful boy.*

CLOWN (*poking* PANTALOON *with his cane*).
Who can this miserable ancient man be?
(*Visited at last by some one who
knows him,* PANTALOON *rises in a
surge of joy.*)

PANTALOON. You have come back, Joey,
after all these years!

CLOWN. Hands off. I came here, my good
fellow, to inquire for a Mr. Joseph.

PANTALOON (*shuddering*). Yes, that's me;
that's all that's left of me; Mr. Joseph!
Me that used to be Joey.

CLOWN. I think I knew you once, Mr.
Joseph?

PANTALOON. Joey, you're hard on me. It
wasn't my fault that Boy tricked us and
ran off wi' her.

CLOWN. May I ask, Mr. Joseph, were you
ever on the boards?

PANTALOON. This to me as was your right
hand!

CLOWN. I seem to call to mind something
like you as used to play the swell.

PANTALOON (*fiercely*). It's a lie! I was
born a Pantaloon, and a Pantaloon I'll die.

CLOWN. Yes, I heard you was dead, Mr.
Joseph. Everybody knows it except
yourself. (*He gnaws a sausage.*)

PANTALOON (*greedily*). Gie me a bite, Joey.

CLOWN (*relentless*). I only bites with the profession. I never bites with the public.

PANTALOON. What brought you here? Just to rub it in?

CLOWN. Let's say I came to make inquiries after the happy pair.

PANTALOON. It's years and years, Joey, since they ran away, and I've never seen them since.

CLOWN. Heard of them?

PANTALOON. Yes, I've heard. They're in distant parts.

CLOWN. Answer their letters?

PANTALOON (*darkening*). No.

CLOWN. They will be doing well, Mr. Joseph, without me?

PANTALOON (*boastfully*). At first they did badly, but when the managers heard Fairy was my daughter they said the daughter o' such a famous old 'un was sure to draw by reason of her father's

name. And they print the name of her
father in big letters.

CLOWN (*rapping it out*). It's you that lie
now. I know about them. They go
starving like vagabonds from town to
town.

PANTALOON. Ay, it's true. They write that
they're starving.

CLOWN. And they've got a kid to add to
their misery. All vagabonds, father,
mother, and kid.

PANTALOON. Rub it in, Joey.

CLOWN. You looks as if you would soon be
starving too.

PANTALOON (*not without dignity*). I'm
pinched.

CLOWN. Well, well, I'm a kindly soul, and
what brought me here was to make you
an offer.

PANTALOON (*glistening*). A shop?

CLOWN. For old times' sake.

PANTALOON (*with indecent eagerness*). To be
old 'un again?

CLOWN. No, you crock, but to carry a sand-
wich-board in the street wi' my new old
'un's name on it.

  (*Pantaloon raises his withered arm,
   but he lets it fall.*)

PANTALOON. May you be forgiven for that,
Joey.

CLOWN. Miaw!

PANTALOON (*who is near his end*). Joey,
there stands humbled before you an old
artist.

CLOWN. Never an artist.

PANTALOON (*firmly*). An artist—at present
disengaged.

CLOWN. Forgotten—clean forgotten.

PANTALOON (*bowing his head*). Yes, that's it—
forgotten. Once famous—now forgotten.
Joey, they don't know me even at the
sausage - shop. I am just one of the
public. My worst time is when we should
be going on the stage, and I think I hear
the gallery boys calling for the old 'un—
'Bravo, old 'un'! Then I sort of break

up. I sleep bad o' nights. I think sleep would come to me if I could rub my back on the scenery again. (*He shudders.*) But the days are longer than the nights. I allus see how I am to get through to-day, but I sit thinking and thinking how I am to get through to-morrow.

CLOWN. Poor old crock. Well, so long.

PANTALOON (*offering him the poker*). Joey, gie me one rub before you go—for old times' sake.

CLOWN. You 'll never be rubbed by a clown again, Mr. Joseph.

PANTALOON. Call me Joey once—say 'Goodbye, old 'un'—for old times' sake.

CLOWN. You will never be called Joey or old 'un by a clown again, Mr. Joseph.

(*With a noble gesture* PANTALOON *bids him begone and the* CLOWN *miaws and goes, twisting a sausage in his mouth as if it were a cigar. So he passes from our sight, funny to the last, or never funny, an equally tragic figure.*

PANTALOON *rummages in the wicker
basket among his gods and strokes
them lovingly, a painted goose, his
famous staff, a bladder on a stick.
He does not know that he is hugging
the bladder to his cold breast as he
again crouches by the fire.*

The door opens, and COLUMBINE *and*
HARLEQUIN *peep in, prepared to receive a blow for welcome.   Their faces
are hollow and their clothes in rags,
and, saddest of all, they cannot dance
in.   They walk in like the weary public.*
COLUMBINE *looks as if she could walk
as far as her father's feet, but never
any farther.   With them is the child.
This is the great surprise:* HE IS A
CLOWN. *They sign to the child
to intercede for them, but though only
a baby, he is a clown, and he must
do it in his own way.   He pats his
nose, grins deliciously with the wrong
parts of his face, and dives beneath*

the table. PANTALOON *looks round
and sees his daughter on her knees
before him.*)

PANTALOON. You! Fairy! Come back!
(*For a moment he is to draw her to him,
then he remembers.*) No, I'll have none
of you. It was you as brought me to
this. Begone, I say begone. (*They are
backing meekly to the door.*) Stop a
minute. Little Fairy, is it true—is it
true my Fairy has a kid? (*She nods,
with glistening eyes that say 'Can you put
me out now?' The baby peers from under
the table, and rubs* PANTALOON'S *legs with
the poker. Poor little baby, he is the last
of the clowns, and knows not what is in
store for him.* PANTALOON *trembles, it
is so long since he has been rubbed. He
dare not look down.*) Fairy, is it the kid?
(*She nods again; the moment has come.*)
My Fairy's kid! (*Somehow he has
always taken for granted that his grand-
child is merely a columbine. If the child*

had been something greater they would all
have got a shop again and served under
him.) Oh, Fairy, if only he had been a
clown !

(*Now you see how it is going. The
babe emerges, and he is a clown.*

Just for a moment PANTALOON *cries.
Then the babe is tantalising him
with a sausage.* PANTALOON *revolves
round him like a happy teetotum.
Who so gay now as* COLUMBINE *and*
HARLEQUIN, *dancing merrily as if it
were again the morning? Oh what
a lark is life. Ring down the curtain quickly, Mr. Prompter, before
we see them all swept into the dust-
heap*).

THE TWELVE-POUND LOOK

THE TWELVE–POUND LOOK

IF quite convenient (as they say about cheques) you are to conceive that the scene is laid in your own house, and that HARRY SIMS is you. Perhaps the ornamentation of the house is a trifle ostentatious, but if you cavil at that we are willing to re-decorate: you don't get out of being HARRY SIMS on a mere matter of plush and dados. It pleases us to make him a city man, but (rather than lose you) he can be turned with a scrape of the pen into a K.C., fashionable doctor, Secretary of State, or what you will. We conceive him of a pleasant rotundity with a thick red neck, but we shall waive that point if you know him to be thin.

It is that day in your career when everything went wrong just when everything seemed to be superlatively right.

In HARRY'S *case it was a woman who did the mischief. She came to him in his great hour and told him she did not admire him. Of course he turned her out of the house and was soon himself again, but it spoilt the morning for him. This is the subject of the play, and quite enough too.*

HARRY *is to receive the honour of knighthood in a few days, and we discover him in the sumptuous 'snuggery' of his home in Kensington (or is it Westminster?), rehearsing the ceremony with his wife. They have been at it all the morning, a pleasing occupation.* MRS. SIMS *(as we may call her for the last time, as it were, and strictly as a good-natured joke) is wearing her presentation gown, and personates the august one who is about to dub her* HARRY *knight. She is seated regally. Her jewelled shoulders proclaim aloud her husband's generosity. She must be an extraordinarily proud and happy woman, yet she has a drawn face and shrinking ways as if there were some one near her of whom she is afraid. She*

claps her hands, as the signal to HARRY.
*He enters bowing, and with a graceful
swerve of the leg. He is only partly in
costume, the sword and the real stockings not
having arrived yet. With a gliding motion
that is only delayed while one leg makes up
on the other, he reaches his wife, and, going
on one knee, raises her hand superbly to his
lips. She taps him on the shoulder with a
paper-knife and says huskily, 'Rise, Sir
Harry.' He rises, bows, and glides about
the room, going on his knees to various articles
of furniture, and rises from each a knight.
It is a radiant domestic scene, and* HARRY
*is as dignified as if he knew that royalty was
rehearsing it at the other end.*

SIR HARRY (*complacently*). Did that seem
    all right, eh?

LADY SIMS (*much relieved*). I think perfect.

SIR HARRY. But was it dignified?

LADY SIMS. Oh, very. And it will be still
    more so when you have the sword.

SIR HARRY. The sword will lend it an air.
There are really the five moments—
(*suiting the action to the word*)—the glide
—the dip—the kiss—the tap—and you
back out a knight. It 's short, but it 's
a very beautiful ceremony. (*Kindly*)
Anything you can suggest?

LADY SIMS. No—oh no. (*Nervously, seeing
him pause to kiss the tassel of a cushion*).
You don't think you have practised till
you know what to do almost too well?

> (*He has been in a blissful temper, but
> such niggling criticism would try
> any man.*)

SIR HARRY. I do not. Don't talk nonsense.
Wait till your opinion is asked for.

LADY SIMS (*abashed*). I 'm sorry, Harry.
(*A perfect butler appears and presents a
card.*) 'The Flora Type-Writing Agency.'

SIR HARRY. Ah, yes. I telephoned them
to send some one. A woman, I suppose,
Tombes?

TOMBES. Yes, Sir Harry.

SIR HARRY. Show her in here. (*He has very lately become a stickler for etiquette.*) And, Tombes, strictly speaking, you know, I am not Sir Harry till Thursday.

TOMBES. Beg pardon, sir, but it is such a satisfaction to us.

SIR HARRY (*good-naturedly*). Ah, they like it downstairs, do they?

TOMBES (*unbending*). Especially the females, Sir Harry.

SIR HARRY. Exactly. You can show her in, Tombes. (*The butler departs on his mighty task.*) You can tell the woman what she is wanted for, Emmy, while I change. (*He is too modest to boast about himself, and prefers to keep a wife in the house for that purpose.*) You can tell her the sort of things about me that will come better from you. (*Smiling happily*) You heard what Tombes said, 'Especially the females.' And he is right. Success! The women like it even better than the men. And rightly. For they share. *You* share, *Lady*

Sims. Not a woman will see that gown without being sick with envy of it. I know them. Have all our lady friends in to see it. It will make them ill for a week.

(*These sentiments carry him off light-heartedly, and presently the disturbing element is shown in. She is a mere typist, dressed in uncommonly good taste, but at contemptibly small expense, and she is carrying her typewriter in a friendly way rather than as a badge of slavery, as of course it is. Her eye is clear; and in odd contrast to* LADY SIMS, *she is self-reliant and serene.*)

KATE (*respectfully, but she should have waited to be spoken to*). Good morning, madam.

LADY SIMS (*in her nervous way, and scarcely noticing that the typist is a little too ready with her tongue*). Good morning. (*As a first impression she rather likes the woman, and the woman, though it is scarcely worth mentioning, rather likes her.* LADY SIMS

*has a maid for buttoning and unbuttoning
her, and probably another for waiting on the
maid, and she gazes with a little envy perhaps at a woman who does things for herself.)*
Is that the type-writing machine?

KATE (*who is getting it ready for use*). Yes
(*not 'Yes, madam,' as it ought to be*). I
suppose if I am to work here I may take
this off. I get on better without it. (*She
is referring to her hat.*)

LADY SIMS. Certainly. (*But the hat is
already off.*) I ought to apologise for my
gown. I am to be presented this week,
and I was trying it on. (*Her tone is not
really apologetic. She is rather clinging
to the glory of her gown, wistfully, as if
not absolutely certain, you know, that it is
a glory.*)

KATE. It is beautiful, if I may presume to
say so. (*She frankly admires it. She
probably has a best, and a second best of
her own: that sort of thing.*)

LADY SIMS (*with a flush of pride in the gown*).

Yes, it is very beautiful. (*The beauty of it gives her courage.*) Sit down, please.

KATE (*the sort of woman who would have sat down in any case*). I suppose it is some copying you want done? I got no particulars. I was told to come to this address, but that was all.

LADY SIMS (*almost with the humility of a servant*). Oh, it is not work for me, it is for my husband, and what he needs is not exactly copying. (*Swelling, for she is proud of* HARRY.) He wants a number of letters answered—hundreds of them—letters and telegrams of congratulation.

KATE (*as if it were all in the day's work*). Yes?

LADY SIMS (*remembering that* HARRY *expects every wife to do her duty*). My husband is a remarkable man. He is about to be knighted. (*Pause, but* KATE *does not fall to the floor.*) He is to be knighted for his services to—(*on reflection*)—for his services. (*She is conscious that she is not*

doing HARRY *justice*.) He can explain
it so much better than I can.

KATE (*in her business-like way*). And I am
to answer the congratulations?

LADY SIMS (*afraid that it will be a hard task*).
Yes.

KATE (*blithely*). It is work I have had some
experience of. (*She proceeds to type.*)

LADY SIMS. But you can't begin till you
know what he wants to say.

KATE. Only a specimen letter. Won't it
be the usual thing?

LADY SIMS (*to whom this is a new idea*). Is
there a usual thing?

KATE. Oh, yes.

> (*She continues to type, and* LADY SIMS,
> *half-mesmerised, gazes at her nimble
> fingers. The useless woman watches
> the useful one, and she sighs, she could
> not tell why.*)

LADY SIMS. How quickly you do it! It
must be delightful to be able to do something, and to do it well.

KATE (*thankfully*). Yes, it is delightful.

LADY SIMS (*again remembering the source of all her greatness*). But, excuse me, I don't think that will be any use. My husband wants me to explain to you that his is an exceptional case. He did not try to get this honour in any way. It was a complete surprise to him——

KATE (*who is a practical Kate and no dealer in sarcasm*). That is what I have written.

LADY SIMS (*in whom sarcasm would meet a dead wall*). But how could you know?

KATE. I only guessed.

LADY SIMS. Is that the usual thing?

KATE. Oh, yes.

LADY SIMS. They don't try to get it?

KATE. I don't know. That is what we are told to say in the letters.

> (*To her at present the only important thing about the letters is that they are ten shillings the hundred.*)

LADY SIMS (*returning to surer ground*). I should explain that my husband is not a man who cares for honours. So long as he does his duty——

KATE. Yes, I have been putting that in.

LADY SIMS. Have you? But he particularly wants it to be known that he would have declined a title were it not——

KATE. I have got it here.

LADY SIMS. What have you got?

KATE (*reading*). 'Indeed, I would have asked to be allowed to decline had it not been that I want to please my wife.'

LADY SIMS (*heavily*). But how could you know it was that?

KATE. Is it?

LADY SIMS (*who after all is the one with the right to ask questions*). Do they all accept it for that reason?

KATE. That is what we are told to say in the letters.

LADY SIMS (*thoughtlessly*). It is quite as if you knew my husband.

KATE. I assure you, I don't even know his name.

LADY SIMS (*suddenly showing that she knows him*). Oh, he wouldn't like that!

> (*And it is here that* HARRY *re-enters in his city garments, looking so gay, feeling so jolly that we bleed for him. However, the annoying* KATHERINE *is to get a shock also.*)

LADY SIMS. This is the lady, Harry.

SIR HARRY (*shooting his cuffs*). Yes, yes. Good morning, my dear.

> (*Then they see each other, and their mouths open, but not for words. After the first surprise* KATE *seems to find some humour in the situation, but* HARRY *lowers like a thunder-cloud.*)

LADY SIMS (*who has seen nothing*). I have been trying to explain to her——

SIR HARRY. Eh—what? (*He controls himself.*) Leave it to me, Emmy; I'll attend to her.

> (LADY SIMS *goes, with a dread fear that somehow she has vexed her lord,*

and then HARRY *attends to the in-
truder.*)

SIR HARRY (*with concentrated scorn*). You!

KATE (*as if agreeing with him*). Yes, it's
funny.

SIR HARRY. The shamelessness of your daring
to come here.

KATE. Believe me, it is not less a surprise
to me than it is to you. I was sent here
in the ordinary way of business. I was
given only the number of the house. I
was not told the name.

SIR HARRY (*withering her*). The ordinary
way of business! This is what you have
fallen to—a typist!

KATE (*unwithered*). Think of it!

SIR HARRY. After going through worse
straits, I'll be bound.

KATE (*with some grim memories*). Much
worse straits.

SIR HARRY (*alas, laughing coarsely*). My
congratulations!

KATE. Thank you, Harry.

SIR HARRY (*who is annoyed, as any man would be, not to find her abject*). Eh? What was that you called me, madam?

KATE. Isn't it Harry? On my soul, I almost forget.

SIR HARRY. It isn't Harry to you. My name is Sims, if you please.

KATE. Yes, I had not forgotten that. It was my name, too, you see.

SIR HARRY (*in his best manner*). It was your name till you forfeited the right to bear it.

KATE. Exactly.

SIR HARRY (*gloating*). I was furious to find you here, but on second thoughts it pleases me. (*From the depths of his moral nature*) There is a grim ·justice in this.

KATE (*sympathetically*). Tell me?

SIR HARRY. Do you know what you were brought here to do?

KATE. I have just been learning. You

have been made a knight, and I was summoned to answer the messages of congratulation.

SIR HARRY. That's it, that's it.   You come on this day as my servant!

KATE. I, who might have been Lady Sims.

SIR HARRY. And you are her typist instead. And she has four men-servants.   Oh, I am glad you saw her in her presentation gown.

KATE. I wonder if she would let me do her washing, Sir Harry?

(*Her want of taste disgusts him.*)

SIR HARRY (*with dignity*). You can go. The mere thought that only a few flights of stairs separates such as you from my innocent children——

(*He will never know why a new light has come into her face.*)

KATE (*slowly*). You have children?

SIR HARRY (*inflated*). Two.

(*He wonders why she is so long in answering.*)

KATE (*resorting to impertinence*). Such a nice number.

SIR HARRY (*with an extra turn of the screw*). Both boys.

KATE. Successful in everything. Are they like you, Sir Harry?

SIR HARRY (*expanding*). They are very like me.

KATE. That 's nice.

> (*Even on such a subject as this she can be ribald.*)

SIR HARRY. Will you please to go.

KATE. Heigho! What shall I say to my employer?

SIR HARRY. That is no affair of mine.

KATE. What will you say to Lady Sims?

SIR HARRY. I flatter myself that whatever I say, Lady Sims will accept without comment.

> (*She smiles, heaven knows why, unless her next remark explains it.*)

KATE. Still the same Harry.

SIR HARRY. What do you mean?

KATE. Only that you have the old confidence in your profound knowledge of the sex.

SIR HARRY (*beginning to think as little of her intellect as of her morals*). I suppose I know my wife.

KATE (*hopelessly dense*). I suppose so. I was only remembering that you used to think you knew her in the days when I was the lady. (*He is merely wasting his time on her, and he indicates the door. She is not sufficiently the lady to retire worsted.*) Well, good - bye, Sir Harry. Won't you ring, and the four men-servants will show me out?

(*But he hesitates.*)

SIR HARRY (*in spite of himself*). As you are here, there is something I want to get out of you. (*Wishing he could ask it less eagerly.*) Tell me, who was the man?

(*The strange woman—it is evident now that she has always been strange to him—smiles tolerantly.*)

KATE. You never found out?

SIR HARRY. I could never be sure.

KATE (*reflectively*). I thought that would worry you.

SIR HARRY (*sneering*). It 's plain that he soon left you.

KATE. Very soon.

SIR HARRY. As I could have told you. (*But still she surveys him with the smile of Monna Lisa. The badgered man has to entreat.*) Who was he? It was fourteen years ago, and cannot matter to any of us now. Kate, tell me who he was?

> (*It is his first youthful moment, and perhaps because of that she does not wish to hurt him.*)

KATE (*shaking a motherly head*). Better not ask.

SIR HARRY. I do ask. Tell me.

KATE. It is kinder not to tell you.

SIR HARRY (*violently*). Then, by James, it was one of my own pals. Was it Bernard Roche? (*She shakes her head.*) It may have been some one who comes to my house still.

KATE. I think not. (*Reflecting*) Fourteen years! You found my letter that night when you went home?

SIR HARRY (*impatient*). Yes.

KATE. I propped it against the decanters. I thought you would be sure to see it there. It was a room not unlike this, and the furniture was arranged in the same attractive way. How it all comes back to me. Don't you see me, Harry, in hat and cloak, putting the letter there, taking a last look round, and then stealing out into the night to meet——

SIR HARRY. Whom?

KATE. Him. Hours pass, no sound in the room but the tick-tack of the clock, and then about midnight you return alone. You take——

SIR HENRY (*gruffly*). I wasn't alone.

KATE (*the picture spoilt*). No? oh. (*Plain-*

tively) Here have I all these years been conceiving it wrongly. (*She studies his face.*) I believe something interesting happened?

SIR HARRY (*growling*). Something confoundedly annoying.

KATE (*coaxing*). Do tell me.

SIR HARRY. We won't go into that. Who was the man? Surely a husband has a right to know with whom his wife bolted.

KATE (*who is detestably ready with her tongue*). Surely the wife has a right to know how he took it. (*The woman's love of bargaining comes to her aid.*) A fair exchange. You tell me what happened, and I will tell you who he was.

SIR HARRY. You will? Very well. (*It is the first point on which they have agreed, and, forgetting himself, he takes a place beside her on the fire-seat. He is thinking only of what he is to tell her, but she, woman-like, is conscious of their proximity.*)

KATE (*tastelessly*). Quite like old times. (*He*

moves away from her indignantly.) **Go
on, Harry.**

SIR HARRY (*who has a manful shrinking from
saying anything that is to his disadvantage*).
Well, as you know, I was dining at the
club that night.

KATE. Yes.

SIR HARRY. Jack Lamb drove me home.
Mabbett Green was with us, and I asked
them to come in for a few minutes.

KATE. Jack Lamb, Mabbett Green? I
think I remember them. Jack was in
Parliament.

SIR HARRY. No, that was Mabbett. They
came into the house with me and—(*with
sudden horror*)—was it him?

KATE (*bewildered*). Who?

SIR HARRY. Mabbett?

KATE. What?

SIR HARRY. The man?

KATE. What man? (*understanding*) Oh no.
I thought you said he came into the house
with you.

SIR HARRY. It might have been a blind.

KATE. Well, it wasn't.   Go on.

SIR HARRY. They came in to finish a talk
we had been having at the club.

KATE. An interesting talk, evidently.

SIR HARRY. The papers had been full that
evening of the elopement of some countess
woman with a fiddler. What was her
name?

KATE. Does it matter?

SIR HARRY. No. (*Thus ends the countess.*)
We had been discussing the thing and—
(*he pulls a wry face*)—and I had been
rather warm——

KATE (*with horrid relish*). I begin to see.
You had been saying it served the hus-
band right, that the man who could not
look after his wife deserved to lose her.
It was one of your favourite subjects.
Oh, Harry, say it was that!

SIR HARRY (*sourly*). It may have been
something like that.

KATE. And all the time the letter was there,

waiting; and none of you knew except
the clock. Harry, it is sweet of you to
tell me. (*His face is not sweet. The
illiterate woman has used the wrong ad-
jective.*) I forget what I said precisely
in the letter.

SIR HARRY (*pulverising her*). So do I. But
I have it still.

KATE (*not pulverised*). Do let me see it
again. (*She has observed his eye wandering to the desk.*)

SIR HARRY. You are welcome to it as a
gift. (*The fateful letter, a poor little dead
thing, is brought to light from a locked
drawer.*)

KATE (*taking it*). Yes, this is it. Harry, how
you did crumple it! (*She reads, not without curiosity.*) 'Dear husband—I call
you that for the last time—I am off. I
am what you call making a bolt of it.
I won't try to excuse myself nor to explain, for you would not accept the ex-
cuses nor understand the explanation.

It will be a little shock to you, but only
to your pride; what will astound you
is that any woman could be such a fool
as to leave such a man as you. I am
taking nothing with me that belongs to
you.   May you be very happy.—Your un-
grateful KATE.   *P.S.*—You need not try
to find out who he is.   You will try, but
you won't succeed.'   (*She folds the nasty
little thing up.*)   I may really have it for
my very own?

SIR HARRY. You really may.

KATE (*impudently*). If you would care for
a typed copy——?

SIR HARRY (*in a voice with which he used to
frighten his grandmother*). None of your
sauce!   (*Wincing*) I had to let them
see it in the end.

KATE. I can picture Jack Lamb eating it.

SIR HARRY. A penniless parson's daughter.

KATE. That is all I was.

SIR HARRY. We searched for the two of
you high and low.

KATE. Private detectives? *but could*

SIR HARRY. They couldn't get on the track of you.

KATE (*smiling*). No?

SIR HARRY. But at last the courts let me serve the papers by advertisement on a man unknown, and I got my freedom.

KATE. So I saw. It was the last I heard of you.

SIR HARRY (*each word a blow for her*). And I married again just as soon as ever I could.

KATE. They say that is always a compliment to the first wife.

SIR HARRY (*violently*). I showed them.

KATE. You soon let them see that if one woman was a fool, you still had the pick of the basket to choose from.

SIR HARRY. By James, I did.

KATE (*bringing him to earth again*). But still, you wondered who he was.

SIR HARRY. I suspected everybody—even my pals. I felt like jumping at their throats and crying, 'It 's you!'

KATE. You had been so admirable to me,
an instinct told you that I was sure to
choose another of the same.

SIR HARRY. I thought, it can't be money,
so it must be looks. Some dolly face.
(*He stares at her in perplexity.*)   He must
have had something wonderful about
him to make you willing to give up all
that you had with me.

KATE (*as if he was the stupid one*). Poor
Harry.

SIR HARRY. And it couldn't have been
going on for long, for I would have
noticed the change in you.

KATE. Would you?

SIR HARRY. I knew you so well.

KATE. You amazing man.

SIR HARRY. So who was he?   Out with it.

KATE. You are determined to know?

SIR HARRY. Your promise.   You gave your
word.

KATE. If I must—— (*She is the villain of the
piece, but it must be conceded that in this*

matter she is reluctant to pain him.) I
am sorry I promised. (*Looking at him
steadily.*) There was no one, Harry; no
one at all.

SIR HARRY (*rising*). If you think you can
play with me——

KATE. I told you that you wouldn't like it.

SIR HARRY (*rasping*). It is unbelievable.

KATE. I suppose it is; but it is true.

SIR HARRY. Your letter itself gives you the lie.

KATE. That was intentional. I saw that
if the truth were known you might have
a difficulty in getting your freedom; and
as I was getting mine it seemed fair that
you should have yours also. So I wrote
my good-bye in words that would be
taken to mean what you thought they
meant, and I knew the law would back
you in your opinion. For the law, like
you, Harry, has a profound understanding of women.

SIR HARRY (*trying to straighten himself*). I
don't believe you yet.

KATE (*looking not unkindly into the soul of this man*). Perhaps that is the best way to take it. It is less unflattering than the truth. But you were the only one. (*Summing up her life.*)   You sufficed.

SIR HARRY. Then what mad impulse——

KATE. It was no impulse, Harry. I had thought it out for a year.

SIR HARRY. A year? (*dazed*).   One would think to hear you that I hadn't been a good husband to you.

KATE (*with a sad smile*). You were a good husband according to your lights.

SIR HARRY (*stoutly*). *I* think so.

KATE. And a moral man, and chatty, and quite the philanthropist.

SIR HARRY (*on sure ground*). All women envied you.

KATE. How you loved me to be envied.

SIR HARRY. I swaddled you in luxury.

KATE (*making her great revelation*). That was it.

SIR HARRY (*blankly*). What?

KATE (*who can be serene because it is all over*). How you beamed at me when I sat at the head of your fat dinners in my fat jewellery, surrounded by our fat friends.

SIR HARRY (*aggrieved*). They weren't so fat.

KATE (*a side issue*). All except those who were so thin. Have you ever noticed, Harry, that many jewels make women either incredibly fat or incredibly thin?

SIR HARRY (*shouting*). I have not. (*Is it worth while to argue with her any longer?*) We had all the most interesting society of the day. It wasn't only business men. There were politicians, painters, writers——

KATE. Only the glorious, dazzling successes. Oh, the fat talk while we ate too much —about who had made a hit and who was slipping back, and what the noo house cost and the noo motor and the gold soup-plates, and who was to be the noo knight.

SIR HARRY (*who it will be observed is un-answerable from first to last*). Was any-

body getting on better than me, and
consequently you?

KATE. Consequently me! Oh, Harry, you
and your sublime religion.

SIR HARRY (*honest heart*). My religion? I
never was one to talk about religion,
but——

KATE. Pooh, Harry, you don't even know
what your religion was and is and will be
till the day of your expensive funeral.
(*And here is the lesson that life has taught
her.*) One's religion is whatever he is
most interested in, and yours is Success.

SIR HARRY (*quoting from his morning paper*).
Ambition—it is the last infirmity of noble
minds.

KATE. Noble minds!

SIR HARRY (*at last grasping what she is talking about*). You are not saying that you
left me because of my success?

KATE. Yes, that was it. (*And now she
stands revealed to him.*) I couldn't en-
dure it. If a failure had come now and

then—but your success was suffocating
me. (*She is rigid with emotion.*) The
passionate craving I had to be done with
it, to find myself among people who had
not got on.

SIR HARRY (*with proper spirit*). There are
plenty of them.

KATE. There were none in our set. When
they began to go down-hill they rolled
out of our sight.

SIR HARRY (*clenching it*). I tell you I am
worth a quarter of a million.

KATE (*unabashed*). That is what you are
worth to yourself. I 'll tell you what
you are worth to me: exactly twelve
pounds. For I made up my mind that
I could launch myself on the world alone
if I first proved my mettle by earning
twelve pounds; and as soon as I had
earned it I left you.

SIR HARRY (*in the scales*). Twelve pounds!

KATE. That is your value to a woman. If
she can't make it she has to stick to you.

SIR HARRY (*remembering perhaps a rectory garden*). You valued me at more than that when you married me.

KATE (*seeing it also*). Ah, I didn't know you then. If only you had been a man, Harry.

SIR HARRY. A man? What do you mean by a man?

KATE (*leaving the garden*). Haven't you heard of them? They are something fine; and every woman is loathe to admit to herself that her husband is not one. When she marries, even though she has been a very trivial person, there is in her some vague stirring toward a worthy life, as well as a fear of her capacity for evil. She knows her chance lies in him. If there is something good in him, what is good in her finds it, and they join forces against the baser parts. So I didn't give you up willingly, Harry. I invented all sorts of theories to explain you. Your hardness—I said it was a

fine want of maukishness. Your coarse-
ness—I said it goes with strength. Your
contempt for the weak—I called it virility.
Your want of ideals was clear-sightedness.
Your ignoble views of women—I tried to
think them funny. Oh, I clung to you
to save myself. But I had to let go;
you had only the one quality, Harry,
success; you had it so strong that it
swallowed all the others.

SIR HARRY (*not to be diverted from the main
issue*). How did you earn that twelve
pounds?

KATE. It took me nearly six months; but
I earned it fairly. (*She presses her hand
on the typewriter as lovingly as many a
woman has pressed a rose.*) I learned this.
I hired it and taught myself. I got some
work through a friend, and with my first
twelve pounds I paid for my machine.
Then I considered that I was free to go,
and I went.

SIR HARRY. All this going on in my house

while you were living in the lap of luxury!
(*She nods.*) By God, you were determined.

KATE (*briefly*). By God, I was.

SIR HARRY (*staring*). How you must have
hated me.

KATE (*smiling at the childish word*). Not a
bit—after I saw that there was a way
out. From that hour you amused me,
Harry; I was even sorry for you, for
I saw that you couldn't help yourself.
Success is just a fatal gift.

SIR HARRY. Oh, thank you.

KATE (*thinking, dear friends in front, of you
and me perhaps*). Yes, and some of your
most successful friends knew it.   One or
two of them used to look very sad at
times, as if they thought they might have
come to something if they hadn't got on.

SIR HARRY (*who has a horror of sacrilege*).
The battered crew you live among now—
what are they but folk who have tried
to succeed and failed?

KATE. That's it; they try, but they fail.

SIR HARRY. And always will fail.

KATE. Always. Poor souls—I say of them. Poor soul—they say of me. It keeps us human. That is why I never tire of them.

SIR HARRY (*comprehensively*). Bah! Kate, I tell you I'll be worth half a million yet.

KATE. I'm sure you will. You're getting stout, Harry.

SIR HARRY. No, I'm not.

KATE. What was the name of that fat old fellow who used to fall asleep at our dinner-parties?

SIR HARRY. If you mean Sir William Crackley——

KATE. That was the man. Sir William was to me a perfect picture of the grand success. He had got on so well that he was very, very stout, and when he sat on a chair it was thus (*her hands meeting in front of her*)—as if he were holding his success together. That is what you are working for, Harry. You will have that and the half million about the same time.

SIR HARRY (*who has surely been very patient*). Will you please to leave my house.

KATE (*putting on her gloves, soiled things*). But don't let us part in anger. How do you think I am looking, Harry, compared to the dull, inert thing that used to roll round in your padded carriages?

SIR HARRY (*in masterly fashion*). I forget what you were like. I'm very sure you never could have held a candle to the present Lady Sims.

KATE. That is a picture of her, is it not?

SIR HARRY (*seizing his chance again*). In her wedding-gown. Painted by an R.A.

KATE (*wickedly*). A knight?

SIR HARRY (*deceived*). Yes.

KATE (*who likes* LADY SIMS: *a piece of presumption on her part*). It is a very pretty face.

SIR HARRY (*with the pride of possession*).
Acknowledged to be a beauty everywhere.

KATE. There is a merry look in the eyes, and
character in the chin.

SIR HARRY (*like an auctioneer*). Noted for
her wit.

KATE. All her life before her when that was
painted. It is a *spirituelle* face too.
(*Suddenly she turns on him with anger,
for the first and only time in the play.*)
Oh, Harry, you brute!

SIR HARRY (*staggered*). Eh? What?

KATE. That dear creature capable of becoming a noble wife and mother—she is
the spiritless woman of no account that
I saw here a few minutes ago. I forgive
you for myself, for I escaped, but that
poor lost soul, oh, Harry, Harry.

SIR HARRY (*waving her to the door*). I'll
thank you— If ever there was a woman
proud of her husband and happy in her
married life, that woman is Lady Sims.

KATE. I wonder.

SIR HARRY. Then you needn't wonder.

KATE (*slowly*). If I was a husband—it is my
advice to all of them—I would often
watch my wife quietly to see whether
the twelve-pound look was not coming
into her eyes. Two boys, did you say,
and both like you?

SIR HARRY. What is that to you?

KATE (*with glistening eyes*). I was only
thinking that somewhere there are two
little girls who, when they grow up—the
dear, pretty girls who are all meant for
the men that don't get on! Well, good-
bye, Sir Harry.

SIR HARRY (*showing a little human weakness, it
is to be feared*). Say first that you 're sorry.

KATE. For what?

SIR HARRY. That you left me. Say you
regret it bitterly. You know you do.
(*She smiles and shakes her head. He is
pettish. He makes a terrible announce-
ment.*) You have spoilt the day for me.

KATE (*to hearten him*). I am sorry for that;

but it is only a pin-prick, Harry. I
suppose it is a little jarring in the moment
of your triumph to find that there is—
one old friend—who does not think you
a success; but you will soon forget it.
Who cares what a typist thinks?

SIR HARRY (*heartened*). Nobody. A typist
at eighteen shillings a week!

KATE (*proudly*). Not a bit of it, Harry. I
double that.

SIR HARRY (*neatly*). Magnificent!

    (*There is a timid knock at the door.*)

LADY SIMS. May I come in?

SIR HARRY (*rather appealingly*). It is Lady
Sims.

KATE. I won't tell. She is afraid to come into
her husband's room without knocking!

SIR HARRY. She is not. (*Uxoriously*) Come
in, dearest. (*Dearest enters carrying the
sword. She might have had the sense not to
bring it in while this annoying person is
here.*)

LADY SIMS (*thinking she has brought her wel-*

come with her). Harry, the sword has come.

SIR HARRY (*who will dote on it presently*). Oh, all right.

LADY SIMS. But I thought you were so eager to practise with it.

> (*The person smiles at this. He wishes he had not looked to see if she was smiling.*)

SIR HARRY (*sharply*). Put it down.

> (LADY SIMS *flushes a little as she lays the sword aside.*)

KATE (*with her confounded courtesy*). It is a beautiful sword, if I may say so.

LADY SIMS (*helped*). Yes.

> (*The person thinks she can put him in the wrong, does she? He'll show her.*)

SIR HARRY (*with one eye on* KATE). Emmy, the one thing your neck needs is more jewels.

LADY SIMS (*faltering*). More!

SIR HARRY. Some ropes of pearls. I'll see

to it. It's a bagatelle to me. (KATE *conceals her chagrin, so she had better be shown the door. He rings.*) I won't detain you any longer, miss.

KATE. Thank you.

LADY SIMS. Going already? You have been very quick.

SIR HARRY. The person doesn't suit, Emmy.

LADY SIMS. I'm sorry.

KATE. So am I, madam, but it can't be helped. Good-bye, your ladyship—good-bye, Sir Harry. (*There is a suspicion of an impertinent curtsey, and she is escorted off the premises by* TOMBES. *The air of the room is purified by her going.* SIR HARRY *notices it at once.*)

LADY SIMS (*whose tendency is to say the wrong thing*). She seemed such a capable woman.

SIR HARRY (*on his hearth*). I don't like her style at all.

LADY SIMS (*meekly*). Of course you know best. (*This is the right kind of woman.*)

SIR HARRY (*rather anxious for corroboration*).
Lord, how she winced when I said I was
to give you those ropes of pearls.

LADY SIMS. Did she? I didn't notice. I
suppose so.

SIR HARRY (*frowning*). Suppose? Surely
I know enough about women to know
that.

LADY SIMS. Yes, oh yes.

SIR HARRY. (*Odd that so confident a man should
ask this.*) Emmy, I know you well, don't
I? I can read you like a book, eh?

LADY SIMS (*nervously*). Yes, Harry.

SIR HARRY (*jovially, but with an inquiring
eye*). What a different existence yours is
from that poor lonely wretch's.

LADY SIMS. Yes, but she has a very con-
tented face.

SIR HARRY (*with a stamp of his foot*). All put
on.   What?

LADY SIMS (*timidly*). I didn't say anything.

SIR HARRY (*snapping*). One would think you
envied her.

LADY SIMS. Envied? Oh no—but I thought she looked so alive. It was while she was working the machine.

SIR HARRY. Alive! That 's no life. It is you that are alive. (*Curtly*) I 'm busy, Emmy. (*He sits at his writing-table.*)

LADY SIMS (*dutifully*). I 'm sorry; I 'll go, Harry (*inconsequentially*). Are they very expensive?

SIR HARRY. What?

LADY SIMS. Those machines?

(*When she has gone the possible meaning of her question startles him. The curtain hides him from us, but we may be sure that he will soon be bland again. We have a comfortable feeling, you and I, that there is nothing of* HARRY SIMS *in us.*)

ROSALIND

The Characters in the play are

Dame Quickly - in whose
pleasant cottage by the sea
the scene is set - played by
Mrs. John Miller.

Charles Roche - a young man
upon whose forehead Public
School (and the particular one)
is written, and almost nothing
else. He is modest and clear
eyed, and would king for
his tub in Paradise. Whatever
you, as his host, ask him to do
he says he would like to
awfully, if you don't mind
his being a priceless duffer
at it. His brain is quite as
good as another's but as yet
he has referred scarcely
any thing to it. He has
not yet decided whether to
drop into business or
diplomacy or the bar and
all unknown to him there
is a grim piece of waste
land waiting for him
in Canada, which he will
make a hash of, or it will
make a man of him. Played
by Mr. Robert

ROSALIND

Two middle-aged ladies are drinking tea in the parlour of a cottage by the sea. It is far from London, and a hundred yards from the cry of children, of whom middle-aged ladies have often had enough. Were the room MRS. *has*
PAGE'S we should make a journey through it in search of character, but she is only a bird of passage; nothing of herself here that has not strayed from her bedroom except some which cushions and rugs: touches of character after all maybe, for they suggest that MRS. PAGE *likes to sit soft.*

The exterior of the cottage is probably picturesque, with a thatched roof, but we shall never know for certain, it being against the rules of the game to step outside and look. The old bowed window of the parlour is of the engaging kind that still brings some carriage folk

89

to a sudden stop in villages, not necessarily to sample the sweets of yester-year exposed within in bottles; its panes are leaded; but MRS. QUICKLY *will put something more modern in their place if ever her ship comes home. They will then be used as the roof of the hen-coop, and ultimately some lovely lady, given, like the chickens, to 'picking up things,' may survey the world through them from a window in Mayfair. The parlour is, by accident, like some woman's face that scores by being out of draw-ing. At present the window is her smile, but one cannot fix features to the haphazard floor, nor to the irregular walls, which neverthe-less are part of the invitation to come and stay here. There are two absurd steps leading up to* MRS. PAGE'S *bedroom, and perhaps they are what give the room its retroussée touch. There is a smell of sea-weed; twice a day Neptune comes gallantly to the window and hands* MRS. PAGE *the smell of sea-weed. He knows probably that she does not like to have to go far for her sea-weed. Perhaps he also suspects her to be something of a spark, and looks forward to his evening visits, of which we know nothing.*

This is a mere suggestion that there may be more in MRS. PAGE (when the moon is up, say) than meets the eye, but we see at present only what does meet the eye as she gossips with her landlady at the tea-table. Is she good-looking? is the universal shriek; the one question on the one subject that really thrills humanity. But the question seems beside the point about this particular lady, who has so obviously ceased to have any interest in the answer. To us who have a few moments to sum her up while she is still at the tea-table (just time enough for sharp ones to form a wrong impression), she is an indolent, sloppy thing, this MRS. PAGE of London, decidedly too plump, and averse to pulling the strings that might contract her; as MRS. QUICKLY may have said, she has let her figure go and snapped her fingers at it as it went. Her hair is braided back at a minimum of labour (and the brush has been left on the parlour mantelpiece). She wears at tea-time a loose and dowdy dressing-gown and large flat slippers. Such a lazy woman (shall we venture?) that if she were a beggar and you offered her alms, she would ask you to put them in her pocket for her.

Yet we notice, as contrary to her type, that she is not only dowdy but self-consciously enamoured of her dowdiness, has a kiss for it so to speak. This is odd, and perhaps we had better have another look at her. The thing waggling gaily beneath the table is one of her feet, from which the sprawling slipper has dropped, to remain where it fell. It is an uncommonly pretty foot, and one instantly wonders what might not the rest of her be like if it also escaped from its moorings.

The foot returns into custody, without its owner having to stoop, and MRS. PAGE *crosses with cheerful languor to a chair by the fire. She has a drawling walk that fits her gown. There is no footstool within reach, and she pulls another chair to her with her feet and rests them on it contentedly. The slippers almost hide her from our view.*

DAME QUICKLY. You Mrs. Cosy Comfort.

MRS. PAGE (*whose voice is as lazy as her walk*). That's what I am. Perhaps a still better name for me would be Mrs. Treacly Contentment. Dame, you like me, don't you? Come here, and tell me why.

DAME. What do I like you for, Mrs. Page? Well, for one thing, it's very kind of you to let me sit here drinking tea and gossiping with you, for all the world as if I were your equal. And for another, you always pay your book the day I bring it to you, and that is enough to make any poor woman like her lodger.

MRS. PAGE. Oh, as a lodger I know I'm well enough, and I love our gossips over the tea-pot, but that is not exactly what I meant. Let me put it in this way: If you tell me what you most envy in me, I shall tell you what I most envy in you.

DAME (*with no need to reflect*). Well, most of all, ma'am, I think I envy you your contentment with middle-age.

MRS. PAGE (*purring*). I am middle-aged, so why should I complain of it?

DAME (*who feels that only yesterday she was driving the youths to desperation*). You even say it as if it were a pretty word.

MRS. PAGE. But isn't it?

DAME. Not when you are up to the knees in it, as I am.

MRS. PAGE. And as I am. But I dote on it. It is such a comfy, sloppy, pull-the-curtains, carpet-slipper sort of word. When I wake in the morning, Dame, and am about to leap out of bed like the girl I once was, I suddenly remember, and I cry 'Hurrah, I 'm middle-aged.'

DAME. You just dumbfounder me when you tell me things like that. (*Here is something she has long wanted to ask.*) You

can't be more than forty, if I may make
so bold?

MRS. PAGE. I am forty and a bittock, as the
Scotch say. That means forty, and a
good wee bit more.

DAME. There! And you can say it without
blinking.

MRS. PAGE. Why not? Do you think I
should call myself a 30-to-45, like a
motor-car? Now what I think I
envy you for most is for being a grandmamma.

DAME (*smiling tolerantly at some picture the
words have called up*). That's a cheap
honour.

MRS. PAGE (*summing up probably her whole
conception of the duties of a grandmother*).
I should love to be a grandmamma, and
toss little toddlekins in the air.

DAME (*who knows that there is more in it than
that*). I dare say you will be some day.

(*The eyes of both turn to a photograph
on the mantelpiece. It represents*

*a pretty woman in the dress of Rosa-
lind.　The* DAME *fingers it for the
hundredth time, and* MRS. PAGE
regards her tranquilly.)

DAME. No one can deny but your daughter
is a pretty piece.　How old will she be
now?

MRS. PAGE.　Dame, I don't know very
much about the stage, but I do know
that you should never, never ask an
actress's age.

DAME.　Surely when they are as young and
famous as this puss is.

MRS. PAGE. She is getting on, you know.
Shall we say twenty-three?

DAME. Well, well, it's true you might be
a grandmother by now.　I wonder she
doesn't marry.　Where is she now?

MRS. PAGE. At Monte Carlo, the papers say.
It is a place where people gamble.

DAME (*shaking her head*).　Gamble?　Dear,
dear, that's terrible.　(*But she knows of
a woman who once won a dinner service*

*without anything untoward happening after-
wards.)* And yet I would like just once
to put on my shilling with the best of
them. If I were you I would try a
month at that place with her.

MRS. PAGE. Not I, I am just Mrs. Cosy Comfort. At Monte Carlo I should be a fish
out of water, Dame, as much as Beatrice
would be if she were to try a month down
here with me.

DAME (*less in disparagement of local society
than of that sullen bore the sea, and bliss-
fully unaware that it intrudes even at
Monte Carlo*). Yes, I'm thinking she
would find this a dull hole. (*In the
spirit of adventure that has carried the
English far*) And yet, play-actress
though she be, I would like to see her,
God forgive me.

    (*She is trimming the lamp when there
     is a knock at the door. She is
     pleasantly flustered, and indicates
     with a gesture that something is con-*

stantly *happening in this go-ahead*
village.)

DAME. It has a visitor's sound.

(*The lodger is so impressed that she*
takes her feet off the chair. Thus
may MRS. QUICKLY'S *ancestors have*
stared at each other in this very
cottage a hundred years ago when
they thought they heard Napoleon
tapping.)

MRS. PAGE (*keeping her head*). If it is the
doctor's lady, she ~~wants to arrange~~
with me about the cutting out for the
mothers' meeting.

DAME (*who has long ceased to benefit from*
these gatherings). Drat the mothers'
meetings.

MRS. PAGE. Oh no, I dote on them. (*She*
is splendidly active; in short, the spirited
woman has got up.) Still, I want my
~~evening snooze now,~~ so just tell her I am
lying down.

DAME (*thankful to be in a plot*). I will.

Mrs. Page. Yes, but let me lie down first,
so that it won't be a fib.

Dame. There, there. That's such a middle
aged thing to say.

(*In the most middle-aged way* Mrs.
Page *spreads herself on a couch.
They have been speaking in a
whisper, and as the* Dame *goes to the
door we have just time to take note
that* Mrs. Quickly *whispered most
beautifully: a softer whisper than
the* Dame's, *but so clear that it might
be heard across a field. This is the
most tell-tale thing we have discovered
about her as yet.*

Before Mrs. Quickly *has reached the
door it opens to admit an impatient
young man in knickerbockers and a
Norfolk jacket, all aglow with rain-
drops. Public school (and the particular one) is written on his forehead,
and almost nothing else; he has
scarcely yet begun to surmise that any-*

thing else may be required. *He is*
modest and clear-eyed, and would ring
for his tub in Paradise; (reputably
athletic also), with an instant smile
always in reserve for the antagonist
who accidentally shins him. Whatever
you, as his host, ask him to do, he says
he would like to awfully if you don't
mind his being a priceless duffer at it;
his vocabulary is scanty, and in his
engaging mouth 'priceless' sums up
all that is to be known of good or ill
in our varied existence; at a pinch it
would suffice him for most of his simple
wants, just as one may traverse the con-
tinent with Combien? His brain is
quite as good as another's, but as yet
he has referred scarcely anything to
it. He respects learning in the aged,
but shrinks uncomfortably from it in
contemporaries, as persons who have
somehow failed. To him the proper
way to look upon ability is as some-

thing we must all come to in the end.
He has a nice taste in the arts that
has come to him by the way of socks,
spats and slips, and of these he has
a large and happy collection, which
he laughs at jollily in public (for his
sense of humour is sufficient), but in
the privacy of his chamber he sometimes spreads them out like troutlet
on the river's bank and has his quiet
thrills of exultation. ~~Having lately~~
left Oxford, *and* ~~he~~ is facing the world
confidently ~~with nothing to impress
it except these and a scarf he won at
Fives (beating Hon. Billy Minhorn)~~.
He has not yet decided whether to drop
into business or diplomacy or the bar.
~~(There will be a lot of fag about this);~~
but ~~and~~ all unknown to him there is a grim
piece of waste land waiting for him in
Canada, which he will make a hash
of, or it will make a man of him
~~Billy will be there too~~.)

CHARLES (*on the threshold*). I beg your pardon awfully, but I knocked three times.

DAME (*liking the manner of him, and indeed it is the nicest manner in the world*). What's your pleasure?

CHARLES. You see how jolly wet my things are. (*These boys get on delightful terms of intimacy at once.*) I am on a walking tour —not that I have walked much—(*they never boast; he has really walked well and far*)— and I got caught in that shower. I thought when I saw a house that you might be kind enough to let me take my jacket off and warm my paws, until I can catch a train.

DAME (*unable to whisper to* MRS. PAGE '*He is good-looking*'). I'm sorry, sir, but I have let the kitchen fire out.

CHARLES (*peeping over her shoulder*). This fire——?

DAME. This is my lodger's room.

CHARLES. Ah, I see. Still, I dare say that if he knew—— (*He has edged farther*

into the room, and becomes aware that there is a lady with eyes closed on the sofa.) I beg your pardon; I didn't know there was any one here.

> *(But the lady on the sofa replies not, and to the* DAME *this is his dismissal.)*

DAME. The station is just round the corner, and there is a waiting-room there.

CHARLES. A station waiting-room fire; I know them. Is she asleep?

DAME. Yes.

CHARLES *(who nearly always gets round them when he pouts)*. Then can't I stay? I won't disturb her.

DAME *(obdurate)*. I'm sorry.

CHARLES *(cheerily—he will probably do well on that fruit-farm)*. Heigho! Well, here is for the station waiting-room.

> *(And he is about to go when* MRS. PAGE *signs to the* DAME *that he may stay. We have given the talk between the* DAME *and* CHARLES *in*

*order to get it over, but our sterner
eye is all the time on* MRS. PAGE.
*Her eyes remain closed as if in sleep
and she is on the sofa prone, yet for the
first time since the curtain rose she
has come to life. As if she knew we
were watching her she is again inert,
but there was a twitch of the mouth a
moment ago that let a sunbeam loose
upon her face. It is gone already,
popped out of the box and returned
to it with the speed of thought. Noticeable as is* MRS. PAGE'S *mischievous
smile, far more noticeable is her
control of it. A sudden thought
occurs to us that the face we had
thought stolid is made of elastic.*)

DAME (*cleverly*). After all, if you 're willing
just to sit quietly by the fire and take
a book——

CHARLES. Rather. Any book. Thank you
immensely. (*And in his delightful way
of making himself at home he whips off his*

*knapsack and steps inside the fender.
'He is saucy, thank goodness,' is what the
Dame's glance at Mrs. Page conveys.
That lady's eyelids flicker as if she had
discovered a way of watching Charles
while she slumbers. Anon his eye alights
on the photograph that has already been
the subject of conversation, and he is instantly exclamatory.)*

Dame (*warningly*). Now, you promised not
to speak.

Charles. But that photograph. How funny
you should have it.

Dame (*severely*). Hsh. It's not mine.

Charles (*with his first glance of interest at
the sleeper*). Hers?

(*The eyelids have ceased to flicker. It
is placid Mrs. Page again. Never
was such an inelastic face.*)

Dame. Yes; only don't talk.

Charles. But this is priceless (*gazing at the
photograph*). I must talk. (*He gives his
reason.*) I know her (*a reason that would*

be complimentary to any young lady). It
is Miss Beatrice Page.

DAME (*who knows the creature man*). You
mean you 've seen her?

CHARLES (*youthfully*). I know her quite well.
I have had lunch with her twice. She
is at Monte Carlo just now. (*Swelling*) I
was one of those that saw her off.

DAME. Yes, that 's the place. Read what
is written across her velvet chest.

CHARLES (*deciphering the writing on the
photograph*). 'To darling Mumsy with
heaps of kisses.' (*His eyes gleam. Is
he in the middle of an astonishing adventure?*) You don't tell me— Is that——?

DAME (*as coolly as though she were passing
the butter*). Yes, that 's her mother. And
a sore trial it must have been to her when
her girl took to such a trade.

CHARLES (*waving aside such nonsense*). But I
say, she never spoke to me about a mother.

DAME. The more shame to her.

CHARLES (*deeply versed in the traffic of the*

stage). I mean she is famed as being almost the only actress who doesn't have a mother.

DAME (*bewildered*). What?

CHARLES (*seeing the uselessness of laying pearls before this lady*). Let me have a look at her.

DAME. It is not to be thought of. (*But an unexpected nod from the sleeper indicates that it may be permitted.*) Oh, well, I see no harm in it if you go softly.

> (*He tiptoes to the sofa, but perhaps* MRS. PAGE *is a light sleeper, for she stirs a little, just sufficiently to become more compact, while the slippers rise into startling prominence. Some humorous dream, as it might be, slightly extends her mouth and turns the oval of her face into a round. Her head has sunk into her neck. Simultaneously, as if her circulation were suddenly held up, a shadow passes over her complexion. This is a bad*

copy of the Mrs. Page *we have seen
hitherto, and will give* Charles *a
poor impression of her.*)

Charles (*peering over the slippers*). Yes,
yes, yes.

Dame. Is she like the daughter, think
you?

Charles (*judicially*). In a way, very. Hair's
not so pretty. She's not such a fine
colour. Heavier build, and I should say
not so tall. None of Miss Page's dis-
tinction, nothing *svelte* about her. As
for the feet (*he might almost have said the
palisade*)—the feet—— (*He shudders a
little, and so do the feet.*)

Dame. She is getting on, you see. She is
forty and a bittock.

Charles. A whattock?

Dame (*who has never studied the Doric*). It
may be a whattock.

Charles (*gallantly*). But there's something
nice about her. I could have told she
was her mother anywhere. (*With which*

handsome compliment he returns to the
fire, and MRS. PAGE, *no doubt much grati-*
fied, throws a kiss after him. She also
signs to the DAME *a mischievous desire to*
be left alone with this blade.

DAME (*discreetly*). Well, I 'll leave you, but,
mind, you are not to disturb her.

    (*She goes, with the pleasant feeling*
      that there are two clever women in
      the house; and with wide-open
      eyes MRS. PAGE *watches* CHARLES
      dealing amorously with the photo-
      graph. Soon he returns to her
      side, and her eyes are closed, but
      she does not trouble to repeat the
      trifling with her appearance. She
      probably knows the strength of first
      impressions.)

CHARLES (*murmuring the word as if it were*
sweet music). Mumsy. (*With conviction*)
You lucky mother.

MRS. PAGE (*in a dream*). Is that you,
Beatrice?

(*This makes him skurry away, but he is soon back again, and the soundness of her slumber annoys him.*)

CHARLES (*in a reproachful whisper*). Woman, wake up and talk to me about your daughter.

(*The selfish thing sleeps on, and somewhat gingerly he pulls away the cushion from beneath her head. Nice treatment for a lady. MRS. PAGE starts up, and at first is not quite sure where she is, you know.*)

MRS. PAGE. Why—what——

CHARLES (*contritely*). I am very sorry. I'm afraid I disturbed you.

MRS. PAGE (*blankly*). I don't know you, do I?

CHARLES (*who has his inspirations*). No, madam, but I wish you did.

MRS. PAGE (*making sure that she is still in the DAME'S cottage*). Who are you? and what are you doing here?

CHARLES (*for truth is best*). My name is Roche. I am nobody in particular. I'm just the usual thing; Eton, Oxford, and so to bed—as Pepys would say. I am on a walking tour, on my way to the station, but there is no train till seven, and your landlady let me in out of the rain on the promise that I wouldn't disturb you.

MRS. PAGE (*taking it all in with a woman's quickness*). I see. (*Suddenly*) But you have disturbed me.

CHARLES. I'm sorry.

MRS. PAGE (*with a covert eye on him*). It wasn't really your fault. This cushion slipped from under me, and I woke up.

CHARLES (*manfully*). No, I—I pulled it away.

MRS. PAGE (*indignant*). You did! (*She advances upon him like a stately ship*). Will you please to tell me why?

CHARLES (*feebly*). I didn't mean to pull so hard. (*Then he gallantly leaps into the breach.*) Madam, I felt it was impossible for me to leave this house without first waking you to tell you of the feelings of solemn respect with which I regard you.

MRS. PAGE. Really.

CHARLES. I suppose I consider you the cleverest woman in the world.

MRS. PAGE. On so short an acquaintance?

CHARLES (*lucidly*). I mean, to have had the priceless cleverness to have her——

MRS. PAGE. Have her? (*A light breaks on her.*) My daughter?

CHARLES. Yes, I know her. (*As who should say, Isn't it a jolly world?*)

MRS. PAGE. You know Beatrice personally?

CHARLES (*not surprised that it takes her a little time to get used to the idea*). I assure you I have that honour. (*In one mouthful*) I think she is the most beautiful and the cleverest woman I have ever known.

MRS. PAGE. I thought I was the cleverest.

CHARLES. Yes, indeed; for I think it even cleverer to have had her than to be her.

MRS. PAGE. Dear me. I must wait till I

get a chair before thinking this out. (*A chair means two chairs to her, as we have seen, but she gives the one on which her feet wish to rest to* CHARLES.) You can have this half, Mr.—ah—Mr.——?

CHARLES. Roche.

MRS. PAGE (*resting from her labours of the last minute*). You are so flattering, Mr. Roche, I think you must be an actor yourself.

CHARLES (*succinctly*). No, I'm nothing. My father says I'm just an expense. But when I saw Beatrice's photograph there (*the nice boy pauses a moment because this is the first time he has said the name to her mother; he is taking off his hat to it*) with the inscription on it——

MRS. PAGE. That foolish inscription.

CHARLES (*arrested*). Do you think so?

MRS. PAGE. I mean foolish, because she has quite spoilt the picture by writing across the chest. That beautiful gown ruined.

CHARLES (*fondly tolerant*). They all do it, even across their trousers; the men I mean.

MRS. PAGE (*interested*). Do they? I wonder why.

CHARLES (*remembering now that other people don't do it*). It does seem odd. (*But after all the others are probably missing something.*)

MRS. PAGE (*shaking her wise head*). I know very little about them, but I am afraid they are an odd race.

CHARLES (*who has doted on many of them, though they were usually not sitting at his table*). But very attractive, don't you think? The ladies I mean.

MRS. PAGE (*luxuriously*). I mix so little with them. I am not a Bohemian, you see. Did I tell you that I have never even seen Beatrice act?

CHARLES. You haven't? How very strange. Not even her Rosalind?

MRS. PAGE (*stretching herself*). No. Is it cruel to her?

CHARLES (*giving her one*). Cruel to yourself. (*But this is no policy for an admirer of Miss Page.*) She gave me her photograph as Rosalind. (*Hurriedly*) Not a postcard.

MRS. PAGE (*who is very likely sneering*). With writing across the chest, I 'll be bound.

CHARLES (*stoutly*). Do you think I value it the less for that?

MRS. PAGE (*unblushing*). Oh no, the more. You have it framed on your mantelshelf, haven't you, so that when the other young bloods who are just an expense drop in they may read the pretty words and say, 'Roche, old man, you are going it.'

CHARLES. Do you really think that I——

MRS. PAGE. Pooh, that was what Beatrice expected when she gave it you.

CHARLES. Silence! (*She raises her eyebrows, and he is stricken.*) I beg your pardon, I should have remembered that you are her mother.

MRS. PAGE (*smiling on him*). I beg yours. I

should like to know, Mr. Roche, where you do keep that foolish photograph.

CHARLES (*with a swelling*). Why, here. (*He produces it in a case from an honoured pocket.*) Won't you look at it?

MRS. PAGE (*with proper solemnity*). Yes. It is one I like.

CHARLES (*cocking his head*). It just misses her at her best.

MRS. PAGE. Her best? You mean her way of screwing her nose?

CHARLES (*who was never sent up for good for lucidity—or perhaps he was*). That comes into it. I mean—I mean her naïveté.

MRS. PAGE. Ah yes, her naïveté. I have often seen her practising it before a glass.

CHARLES (*with a disarming smile*). Excuse me; you haven't, you know.

MRS. PAGE (*disarmed*). Haven't I? Well, well, I dare say she is a wonder, but, mind you, when all is said and done, it is for her nose that she gets her salary. May I read what is written on the chest?

(*She reads.*)   The baggage!   (*Shaking her
head at him.*)   But this young lady on
the other side, who is she, Lothario?

CHARLES (*boyish and stumbling*).   That is my
sister.   She died three years ago.   We
were rather—chums—and she gave me
that case to put her picture in.   So
I did.

> (*He jerks it out, glaring at her to see if
> she is despising him.   But* MRS.
> PAGE, *though she cannot be senti-
> mental for long, can be very good at it
> while it lasts.*)

MRS. PAGE (*quite moved*).   Good brother.
And it is a dear face.   But you should not
have put my Beatrice opposite it, Mr.
Roche: your sister would not have liked
that.   It was thoughtless of you.

CHARLES.   My sister would have liked it very
much.   (*Floundering*)   When she gave me
the case she said to me—you know what
girls are—she said, 'If you get to love a
woman, put her picture opposite mine,

and then when the case is closed I shall
be kissing her.'

> (*His face implores her not to think him
> a silly. She is really more troubled
> than we might have expected.*)

MRS. PAGE (*rising*). Mr. Roche, I never
dreamt——

CHARLES. And that is why I keep the two
pictures together.

MRS. PAGE. You shouldn't.

CHARLES. Why shouldn't I? Don't you
dare to say anything to me against my
Beatrice.

MRS. PAGE (*with the smile of ocean on her
face*). Your Beatrice. You poor boy.

CHARLES. Of course I haven't any right to
call her that. I haven't spoken of it to
her yet. I'm such a nobody, you see.
(*Very nice and candid of him, but we may
remember that his love has not set him
trying to make a somebody out of the
nobody. Are you perfectly certain,
CHARLES, that to be seen with the cele-*

brated PAGE *is not almost more delightful to you than to be with her? Her mother at all events gives him the benefit of the doubt, or so we interpret her sudden action. She tears the photograph in two. He protests indignantly.*)

MRS. PAGE. Mr. Roche, be merry and gay with Beatrice as you will, but don't take her seriously. (*She gives him back the case.*) I think you said you had to catch a train.

CHARLES (*surveying his torn treasure. He is very near to tears, but decides rather recklessly to be a strong man*). Not yet; I must speak of her to you now.

MRS. PAGE (*a strong woman without having to decide*). I forbid you.

CHARLES (*who, if he knew himself, might see that a good deal of gloomy entertainment could be got by stopping here and stalking London as the persecuted of his lady's mamma*). I have the right. There is no decent man who hasn't the right to tell a woman that he loves her daughter.

MRS. PAGE (*determined to keep him to earth
though she has to hold him down*). She
doesn't love you, my friend.

CHARLES (*though a hopeless passion would be
another rather jolly thing*). How do you
know? You have already said——

MRS. PAGE (*rather desperate*). I wish you had
never come here.

CHARLES (*manfully*). Why are you so set
against me? I think if I was a woman
I should like at any rate to take a good
straight look into the eyes of a man who
said he was fond of her daughter. You
might have to say 'No' to him, but
often you must have had thoughts of
the kind of man who would one day
take her from you, and though I may
not be the kind, I assure you, I—I am
just as fond of her as if I were. (*Not
bad for* CHARLES. *Sent up for good this
time.*)

MRS. PAGE (*beating her hands together in
distress*). You are torturing me, Charles.

CHARLES. But why? Did I tell you my name was Charles? (*With a happy thought.*) She has spoken of me to you! What did she say?

>   (*If he were thinking less of himself and a little of the woman before him he would see that she has turned into an exquisite supplicant.*)

MRS. PAGE. Oh, boy—you boy! Don't say anything more. Go away now.

CHARLES. I don't understand.

MRS. PAGE. I never had an idea that you cared in that way. I thought we were only jolly friends.

CHARLES. We?

MRS. PAGE (*with a wry lip for the word that has escaped her*). Charles, if you must know, can't you help me out a little? Don't you see at last?

>   (*She has come to him with undulations as lovely as a swallow's flight, mocking, begging, not at all the woman we have been watching; she*

has become suddenly a disdainful,
melting armful. But CHARLES *does*
not see.)

CHARLES (*the obtuse*). I—I——

MRS. PAGE. Very well. But indeed I am
sorry to have to break your pretty toy.
(*Drooping still farther on her stem.*)
Beatrice, Mr. Roche, has not had a
mother this many a year. Do you see
now?

CHARLES. No.

MRS. PAGE. Well, well. (*Abjectly*) Beatrice, Mr. Roche, is forty and a bittock.

CHARLES. I—you—but—oh no.

MRS. PAGE (*for better, for worse*). Yes, I am
Beatrice. (*He looks to the photograph to
rise up and give her the lie.*) The writing
on the photograph? A jest. I can explain that.

CHARLES. But—but it isn't only on the stage
I have seen her. I know her off
too.

MRS. PAGE. A little. I can explain that

also. (*He is a very woeful young man.*)
I am horribly sorry, Charles.

CHARLES (*with his last kick*). Even now——

MRS. PAGE. Do you remember an incident
with a pair of scissors one day last June
in a boat near Maidenhead?

CHARLES. When Beatrice—when you—when
she—cut her wrist?

MRS. PAGE. And you kissed the place to
make it well. It left its mark.

CHARLES. I have seen it since.

MRS. PAGE. You may see it again, Charles.
(*She offers him her wrist, but he does not
look. He knows the mark is there. For
the moment the comic spirit has deserted
her, so anxious is she to help this tragic
boy. She speaks in the cooing voice that
proves her to be Beatrice better than any
wrist-mark.*) Am I so terribly unlike
her as you knew her.

CHARLES (*ah, to be stabbed with the voice you
have loved*). No, you are very like, only
—yes, I know now it's you.

MRS. PAGE (*pricked keenly*). Only I am looking my age to-day. (*Forlorn*) This is my real self, Charles—if I have one. Why don't you laugh, my friend. I am laughing. (*No, not yet, though she will be presently.*) You won't give me away, will you? (*He shakes his head.*) I know you won't now, but it was my first fear when I saw you. (*With a sigh.*) And now, I suppose, I owe you an explanation.

CHARLES (*done with the world*). Not unless you wish to.

MRS. PAGE. Oh yes, I wish to. (*The laughter is bubbling up now.*) Only it will leave you a wiser and a sadder man. You will never be twenty-three again, Charles.

CHARLES (*recalling his distant youth*). No, I know I won't.

MRS. PAGE (*now the laughter is playing round her mouth*). Ah, don't take it so lugubriously. You will only jump to twenty-four, say. (*She sits down beside him to*

make full confession.) You must often
have heard gossip about actresses' ages?

CHARLES. I didn't join in it.

MRS. PAGE. Then you can't be a member of
a club.

CHARLES. If they began it——

MRS. PAGE. You wouldn't listen?

CHARLES. Not about you. I dare say I listened about the others.

MRS. PAGE. You nice boy. And now to
make you twenty-four. (*Involuntarily,
true to the calling she adorns, she makes the
surgeon's action of turning up her sleeves.*)
You have seen lots of plays, Charles?

CHARLES. Yes, tons.

MRS. PAGE. Have you noticed that there are
no parts in them for middle-aged ladies?

CHARLES (*who has had too happy a life to
notice this or almost anything else*). Aren't
there?

MRS. PAGE. Oh no, not for 'stars.' There
is nothing for them between the ages of
twenty-nine and sixty. Occasionally one

of the less experienced dramatists may write such a part, but with a little coaxing we can always make him say, 'She needn't be more than twenty-nine.' And so, dear Charles, we have succeeded in keeping middle-age for women off the stage. Why, even Father Time doesn't let on about us. He waits at the wings with a dark cloth for us, just as our dressers wait with dust-sheets to fling over our expensive frocks; but we have a way with us that makes even Father Time reluctant to cast his cloak; perhaps it is the coquettish imploring look we give him as we dodge him; perhaps though he is an old fellow he can't resist the powder on our pretty noses. And so he says, 'The enchanting baggage, I'll give her another year.' When you come to write my epitaph, Charles, let it be in these delicious words, 'She had a long twenty-nine.'

CHARLES. But off the stage—I knew you off.

(*Recalling a gay phantom*) Why, I was one of those who saw you into your train for Monte Carlo.

MRS. PAGE. You thought you did. That made it easier for me to deceive you here. But I got out of that train at the next station.

> (*She makes a movement to get out of the train here. We begin to note how she suits the action to the word in obedience to Shakespeare's fatal injunction; she cannot mention the tongs without forking two of her fingers.*)

CHARLES. You came here instead?

MRS. PAGE. Yes, stole here.

CHARLES (*surveying the broken pieces of her*). Even now I can scarcely— You who seemed so young and gay.

MRS. PAGE (*who is really very good-natured, else would she clout him on the head*). I was a twenty-nine. Oh, don't look so solemn, Charles. It is not confined to the stage. The stalls are full of twenty-nines. Do you remember what fun it was to help me on with my cloak? Remember why I had to put more powder on my chin one evening?

CHARLES (*with a groan*). It was only a few weeks ago.

MRS. PAGE. ~~Yes. Sometimes it was Mr.~~ Time I saw in the mirror, but the wretch only winked at me and went his way.

CHARLES (*ungallantly*). But your whole appearance—so girlish compared to——

MRS. PAGE (*gallantly*). To this. I am coming to 'this,' Charles. (*Confidentially; no one can be quite so delightfully confidential as* BEATRICE PAGE.) You see, never having been more than twenty-nine, not even in my sleep—for we have to keep it up even in our sleep—I began to wonder what middle-age was like. I wanted to feel the sensation. A woman's curiosity, Charles.

CHARLES. Still, you couldn't——

MRS. PAGE. Couldn't I! Listen. Two

summers ago, instead of going to Biarritz
—see pictures of me in the illustrated
papers stepping into my motor-car, or
going a round of country houses—see
photographs of us all on the steps—the
names, Charles, read from left to right—
instead of doing any of these things I
pretended I went there, and in reality I
came down here, determined for a whole
calendar month to be a middle-aged lady.
I had to get some new clothes, real, cosy,
sloppy, very middle-aged clothes; and
that is why I invented mamma; I got
them for her, you see. I said she was
about my figure, but stouter and shorter,
as you see she is.

CHARLES (*his eyes wandering up and down
her—and nowhere a familiar place*). I can't
make out——

MRS. PAGE. No, you are too nice a boy to
make it out. You don't understand the
difference that a sober way of doing one's
hair, and the letting out of a few strings,

and sundry other trifles that are no trifles, make; but you see I vowed that if the immortal part of me was to get a novel sort of rest, my figure should get it also. *Voila!* And thus all cosy within and without, I took lodgings in the most out-of-the-world spot I knew of, in the hope that here I might find the lady of whom I was in search.

CHARLES. Meaning?

MRS. PAGE (*rather grimly*). Meaning myself. Until two years ago she and I had never met.

CHARLES (*the cynic*). And how do you like her?

MRS. PAGE. Better than you do, young sir. She is really rather nice. I don't suppose I could do with her all the year round, but for a month or so I am just wallowing in her. You remember my entrancing little shoes? (*she wickedly exposes her flapping slippers*). At local dances I sit out deliciously as a wall-flower. Drop a tear, Charles, for me as a wall-flower. I play cards, and the engaged ladies give me their confidences as a dear old thing; and I never, never dream of setting my cap at their swains.

CHARLES. How strange. You who, when you liked——

MRS. PAGE (*plaintively*). Yes, couldn't I, Charles?

CHARLES (*falling into the snare*). It was just the wild gaiety of you.

MRS. PAGE (*who is in the better position to know*). It was the devilry of me.

CHARLES. Whatever it was, it bewitched us.

MRS. PAGE (*candidly, but forgiving herself*). It oughtn't to.

CHARLES. If you weren't all glee you were the saddest thing on earth.

MRS. PAGE. But I shouldn't have been sad on your shoulders, Charles.

CHARLES (*appealing*). You weren't sad on all our shoulders, were you?

MRS. PAGE (*reassuring*). No, not all.

> Oh the gladness of her gladness when she's glad,
> And the sadness of her sadness when she's sad,
> But the gladness of her gladness
> And the sadness of her sadness
> Are as nothing, Charles,
> To the badness of her badness when she's bad.

> (*This dagger-to-her-breast business is
> one of her choicest tricks of fence,
> and is very dangerous if you can coo
> like Beatrice.*)

CHARLES (*pinked*). Not a word against yourself.

MRS. PAGE (*already seeing what she has been up to*). Myself! I suppose even now I am only playing a part.

CHARLES (*who has become her handkerchief*). No, no, this is your real self.

MRS. PAGE (*warily*). Is it? I wonder.

CHARLES. I never knew any one who had deeper feelings.

MRS. PAGE. Oh, I am always ready with whatever feeling is called for. I have a wardrobe of them, Charles. Don't blame me, blame the public of whom you are one; the pitiless public that has made me what I am. I am their slave and their plaything, and when I please them they fling me nuts. (*Her voice breaks, no voice can break so naturally as* BEATRICE'S.) I would have been a darling of a wife— don't you think so, Charles?—but they wouldn't let me. I am only a bundle of emotions; I have two characters for each day of the week. Home became a less thing to me than a new part. Charles, if only I could have been a nobody. Can't you picture me, such a happy, unknown woman, dancing along some sandy shore with half a dozen little boys and girls hanging on to my skirts? When my son was old enough, wouldn't he and I have made a rather pretty picture for the king the day he joined his ship. And I think most of

all I should have loved to deck out my
daughter in her wedding-gown.

> When her mother tends her before the laughing
>   mirror,
> Tying up her laces, looping up her hair—

But the public wouldn't have it, and I
had to pay the price of my success.

CHARLES (*heart-broken for that wet face*).
Beatrice!

MRS. PAGE. I became a harum-scarum,
Charles; sometimes very foolish—(*With
a queer insight into herself*) chiefly
through good-nature I think. There
were moments when there was nothing
I wouldn't do, so long as I was all right
for the play at night. Nothing else
seemed to matter. I have kicked over
all the traces, my friend. You remember
the Scottish poet who

> Keenly felt the friendly glow
>   And softer flame,
> But thoughtless follies laid him low
>   And stained his name.

(*Sadly enough*) Thoughtless follies laid her low, Charles, and stained her name.

CHARLES (*ready to fling down his glove in her defence*). I don't believe it. No, no, Beatrice—Mrs. Page——

MRS. PAGE. Ah, it 's Mrs. Page now.

CHARLES. You are crying.

MRS. PAGE (*with some satisfaction*). Yes, I am crying.

CHARLES. This is terrible to me. I never dreamt your life was such a tragedy.

MRS. PAGE (*coming to*). Don't be so concerned. I am crying, but all the time I am looking at you through the corner of my eye to see if I am doing it well.

CHARLES (*hurt*). Don't—don't.

MRS. PAGE (*well aware that she will always be her best audience*). Soon I 'll be laughing again. When I have cried, Charles, then it is time for me to laugh.

CHARLES. Please, I wish you wouldn't.

MRS. PAGE (*already in the grip of another devil*). And from all this, Charles, you have so nobly offered to save me. You are prepared to take me away from this dreadful life and let me be my real self. (CHARLES *distinctly blushes*.) Charles, it is dear and kind of you, and I accept your offer. (*She gives him a come-and-take-me curtsey and awaits his rapturous response. The referee counts ten, but* CHARLES *has not risen from the floor. Goose that he is; she trills with merriment, though there is a touch of bitterness in it*.) You see the time for laughing has come already. You really thought I wanted you, you conceited boy. (*Rather grandly*) I am not for the likes of you.

CHARLES (*abject*). Don't mock me. I am very unhappy.

MRS. PAGE (*putting her hand on his shoulder in her dangerous, careless, kindly way*). There, there, it is just a game. All life's a game.

(*It is here that the telegram comes.* MRS. QUICKLY *brings it in; and the*

better to read it, but with a glance at
CHARLES *to observe the effect on him,*
MRS. PAGE *puts on her large horn*
spectacles. He sighs.)

DAME. Is there any answer? The girl is
waiting.

MRS. PAGE. No answer, thank you.

> (MRS. QUICKLY *goes, wondering what*
> *those two have had to say to each*
> *other.*)

CHARLES (*glad to be a thousand miles away from*
recent matters). Not bad news, I hope?

MRS. PAGE (*wiping her spectacles*). From
my manager. It is in cipher, but what
it means is that the summer play isn't
drawing, and that they have decided to
revive *As You Like It*. They want me
back to rehearse to-morrow at eleven.

CHARLES (*indignant*). They can't even let you
have a few weeks.

MRS. PAGE (*returning from London*). What?
Heigho, is it not sad? But I had been
warned that this might happen.

CHARLES (*evolving schemes*). Surely if you-—
    (*But she has summoned* MRS. QUICKLY.)

MRS. PAGE (*plaintively*). Alas, Dame, our
    pleasant gossips have ended for this year.
    I am called back to London hurriedly.

DAME. Oh dear, the pity! (*She has already
    asked herself what might be in the telegram.*)
    Your girl has come back, and she wants
    you? Is that it?

MRS. PAGE. That's about it. (*Her quiet,
    sad manner says that we must all dree our
    weird.*) I must go. Have I time to
    catch the express?

CHARLES (*dispirited*). It leaves at seven.

MRS. PAGE (*bravely*). I think I can do it. Is
    that the train you are to take?

CHARLES. Yes, but only to the next station.

MRS. PAGE (*grown humble in her misfortune*).
    Even for that moment of your company
    I shall be grateful. Dame, this gentle-
    man turns out to be a friend of Beatrice.

DAME. So he said, but I suspicioned him.

MRS. PAGE. Well, he is. Mr. Roche, this is

my kind Dame. I must put a few things together.

DAME. If I can help——

MRS. PAGE. You can send on my luggage to-morrow; but here is one thing you might do now. Run down to the Rectory and tell them why I can't be there for the cutting-out.

DAME. I will.

MRS. PAGE. I haven't many minutes. Good-bye, you dear, for I shall be gone before you get back. I 'll write and settle everything. (*With a last look round*) Cosy room! I have had a lovely time.

> (*Her face quivers a little, but she does not break down. She passes, a courageous figure, into the bedroom. The slippers plop as she mounts the steps to it. Her back looks older than we have seen it; at least such is its intention.*)

DAME (*who has learned the uselessness of railing against fate*). Dearie dear, what a pity.

CHARLES (*less experienced*). It's horrible.

DAME (*wisely turning fate into a gossip*). Queer to think of a lady like Mrs. Page having a daughter that jumps about for a living. (*Good God, thinks* CHARLES, *how little this woman knows of life.*) What I sometimes fear is that the daughter doesn't take much care of her. I dare say she's fond of her, but does she do the little kind things for her that a lady come Mrs. Page's age needs?

CHARLES (*wincing*). She's not so old.

DAME (*whose mind is probably running on breakfast in bed and such-like matters*). No, but at our age we are fond of—of quiet, and I doubt she doesn't get it.

CHARLES. I know she doesn't.

DAME (*stumbling among fine words which attract her like a display of drapery*). She says it's her right to be out of the hurly-burly and into what she calls the delicious twilight of middle-age.

CHARLES (*with dizzying thoughts in his brain*).

If she is so fond of it, isn't it a shame
she should have to give it up?

DAME. The living here.

CHARLES. Not so much that as being middle-
aged.

DAME. Give up being middle-aged! How
could she do that?

(*He is saved replying by* MRS. PAGE,
who calls from the bedroom.)

MRS. PAGE. Dame, I hear you talking, and
you promised to go at once.

(*The* DAME *apologises, and is off.*
CHARLES *is left alone with his great
resolve, which is no less than to do
one of the fine things of history. It
carries him toward the bedroom door,
but not quickly; one can also see
that it has a rival who is urging him
to fly the house.*)

CHARLES (*with a drum beating inside him*).
Beatrice, I want to speak to you at once.

MRS. PAGE (*through the closed door*). As soon
as I have packed my bag.

CHARLES (*finely*). Don't pack it.

MRS. PAGE. I must.

CHARLES. I have something to say.

MRS. PAGE. I can hear you.

CHARLES (*who had been honourably mentioned for the school prize poem*). Beatrice, until now I hadn't really known you at all. The girl I was so fond of, there wasn't any such girl.

MRS. PAGE. Oh yes, indeed there was.

CHARLES (*now in full sail for a hero's crown*). There was the dear woman who was Rosalind, but she had tired of it. Rosalind herself grew old and gave up the forest of Arden, but there was one man who never forgot the magic of her being there; and I shall never forget yours. (*Strange that between the beatings of the drum he should hear a little voice within him calling, 'Ass, Charles, you ass!' or words to that effect. But he runs nobly on.*) My dear, I want to be your Orlando to the end. (*Surely nothing could be grander. He is chagrined to get no response beyond what might be the breaking of a string.)* Do you hear me?

MRS. PAGE. Yes. *(A brief answer, but he is off again.)*

CHARLES. I will take you out of that hurly-burly and accompany you into the delicious twilight of middle-age. I shall be staid in manner so as not to look too young, and I will make life easy for you in your declining years. *('Ass, Charles, you ass!')* Beatrice, do come out.

MRS. PAGE. I am coming now. *(She comes out carrying her bag.)* You naughty Charles, I heard you proposing to mamma.

> *(The change that has come over her is far too subtle to have grown out of a wish to surprise him, but its effect on* CHARLES *is as if she had struck him in the face.*
>
> *Too subtle also to be only an affair of clothes, though she is now in bravery hot from Mdme. Make-the-woman*

*tackle by Monsieur, a Rosalind cap
jaunty on her head, her shoes so
small that one wonders if she ever
has to light a candle to look for her
feet. She is a tall, slim young
creature, easily breakable; svelte is
the word that encompasses her as
we watch the flow of her figure, her
head arching on its long stem, and
the erect shoulders that we seem, God
bless us, to remember as a little
hunched. Her eyes dance with life
but are easily startled, because they
are looking fresh upon the world,
wild notes in them as from the woods.
Not a woman this but a maid, or
so it seems to* Charles.

*She has been thinking very little about
him, but is properly gratified by
what she reads in his face.)*

Do I surprise you as much as that,
Charles?

(She puts down her bag, Beatrice

PAGE'S *famous bag. If you do not know it, you do not, alas, know* BEATRICE. *It is seldom out of her hand, save when cavaliers have been sent in search of it. She is always late for everything except her call, and at the last moment she sweeps all that is most precious to her into the bag, and runs. Jewels? Oh no, pooh; letters from nobodies, postal orders for them, a piece of cretonne that must match she forgets what, bits of string she forgets why, a book given her by darling What's-his-name, a broken miniature, part of a watch-chain, a dog's collar, such a neat parcel tied with ribbon (golden gift or biscuits? she means to find out some day), a purse, but not the right one, a bottle of gum without a cork, and a hundred good-natured scatter-brained things besides. Her servants (who all adore her) hate the bag as if it were a little dog; swains hate it because it gets lost and has to be found in the middle of a declaration; managers hate it because she carries it at rehearsals, when it bursts open suddenly like a too tightly laced lady, and its contents are spread on the stage; authors make engaging remarks about it until they discover that it has an artful trick of bursting because she does not know her lines. If you complain, really furious this time, she takes you all in her arms. Well, well, but what we meant to say was that when* BEATRICE *sees* CHARLES'S *surprise she puts down her bag.*)

CHARLES. Good God! Is there nothing real in life?

(*She curves toward him in one of those swallow-flights which will haunt the stage long after* BEATRICE PAGE *is but a memory. What they say and how they said it soon passes*

away; what lives on is the pretty
movements like BEATRICE'S *swallow-*
flights. All else may go, even the
golden voices go, but the pretty move-
ments remain and play about the stage
for ever. They are the only ghosts
of the theatre.)

MRS. PAGE. Heaps of things. Rosalind is
real, and I am Rosalind; and the forest
of Arden is real, and I am going back
to it; and cakes and ale are real, and
I am to eat and drink them again.
Everything is real except middle-age.

(*She puts her hand on his shoulder in*
the old, dangerous, kindly, too friendly
way. That impulsive trick of yours,
madam, has a deal to answer for.)

CHARLES. But you said——

(*She flings up her hands in mockery;*
they are such subtle hands that she
can stand with her back to you, and,
putting them behind her, let them play
the drama.)

Mrs. Page. I said! (*She is gone from him in another flight.*) I am Rosalind and I am going back. Hold me down, Charles, unless you want me to go mad with glee.

Charles (*gripping her*). I feel as if in the room you came out of you have left the woman who went into it five minutes ago.

Mrs. Page (*slipping from him as she slips from all of us*). I have, Charles, I have. I left the floppy, sloppy, old frump in a trunk to be carted to the nearest place where they store furniture; and I tell you, my friend (*she might have said friends, for it is a warning to the Charleses of every age*), if I had a husband and children I would cram them on top of the cart if they sought to come between me and Arden.

Charles (*with a shiver*). Beatrice!

Mrs. Page. The stage is waiting, the audience is calling, and up goes the curtain. Oh, my public, my little dears, come and foot it again in the forest, and tuck away your double chins.

CHARLES. You said you hated the public.

MRS. PAGE. It was mamma said that. They are my slaves and my playthings, and I toss them nuts. (*He knows not how she got there, but for a moment of time her head caressingly skims his shoulder, and she is pouting in his face.*) Every one forgives me but you, Charles, every one but you.

CHARLES (*delirious*). Beatrice, you unutterable delight——

MRS. PAGE (*worlds away*). Don't forgive me if you would rather not.

> Here 's a sigh to those who love me,
> And a smile to those who hate.

CHARLES (*pursuing her*). There is no one like you on earth, Beatrice. Marry me, marry me (*as if he would catch her*).

MRS. PAGE (*cruelly*). As a staff for my declining years?

CHARLES. Forget that rubbish and marry me, you darling girl.

MRS. PAGE. I can't and I won't, but I 'm glad I am your darling girl. (*Very likely she is about to be delightful to him, but suddenly she sees her spoil-sport of a bag.*) I am trusting to you not to let me miss the train.

CHARLES. I am coming with you all the way. (*As if she needed to be told.*) We had better be off.

MRS. PAGE (*seizing the bag*). Charles, as we run to the station we will stop at every telegraph post and carve something sweet on it—'From the East to Western Ind'—

CHARLES (*inspired*). 'No jewel is like Rosalind'—

MRS. PAGE. 'Middle-age is left behind'—

CHARLES. 'For ever young is Rosalind.' Oh, you dear, Motley 's the only wear.

MRS. PAGE. And all the way up in the train, Charles, you shall woo me exquisitely. Nothing will come of it, but you are twenty-three again, and you will have a lovely time.

CHARLES. I 'll win you, I 'll win you.

MRS. PAGE. And eventually you will marry the buxom daughter of the wealthy tallow-chandler——

CHARLES. Never, I swear.

MRS. PAGE (*screwing her nose*). And bring your children to see me playing the Queen in *Hamlet*.

> (*Here* CHARLES ROCHE, *bachelor, kisses the famous* BEATRICE PAGE. *Another sound is heard.*)

CHARLES. The whistle of the train.

MRS. PAGE. Away, away! 'Tis Touchstone calling. Fool, I come, I come. (*To bedroom door*) Ta-ta, mamma.

> (*They are gone.*)

THE WILL

THE WILL

THE *scene is any lawyer's office.*

It may be, and no doubt will be, the minute reproduction of some actual office, with all the characteristic appurtenances thereof, every blot of ink in its proper place; but for the purpose in hand any bare room would do just as well. The only thing essential to the room, save the two men sitting in it, is a framed engraving on the wall of Queen Victoria, which dates sufficiently the opening scene, and will be changed presently to King Edward; afterwards to King George, to indicate the passing of time. No other alteration is called for. Doubtless different furniture came in, and the tiling of the fire-place was renewed, and at last some one discovered that the flowers in the window-box were dead, but all that is as immaterial to the action as the new blue-bottles; the succession of monarchs will convey allegori-

cally the one thing necessary, that time is passing, but that the office of Devizes, Devizes, and Devizes goes on.

The two men are DEVIZES SENIOR *and* JUNIOR. SENIOR, *who is middle-aged, succeeded to a good thing years ago, and as the curtain rises we see him bent over his table making it a better thing. It is pleasant to think that before he speaks he adds another thirteen and fourpence, say, to the fortune of the firm.*

JUNIOR *is quite a gay dog, twenty-three, and we catch him skilfully balancing an office ruler on his nose. He is recently from Oxford—*

If you show him in Hyde Park, lawk, how they will
stare,
Tho' a very smart figure in Bloomsbury Square.

Perhaps JUNIOR *is a smarter figure in the office (among the clerks) than he was at Oxford, but this is one of the few things about him that his shrewd father does not know.*

There moves to them by the only door into the room a middle-aged clerk called SURTEES, *who is perhaps worth looking at, though his manner is that of one who has long ceased to think of himself as of any importance to either God or man. Look at him again, however (which few would do), and you may guess that he has lately had a shock—touched a living wire—and is a little dazed by it. He brings a card to* Mr. Devizes, Senior, *who looks at it and shakes his head.*

Mr. Devizes. 'Mr. Philip Ross.' Don't know him.

Surtees (*who has an expressionless voice*). He says he wrote you two days ago, sir, explaining his business.

Mr. Devizes. I have had no letter from a Philip Ross.

Robert. Nor I.

> (*He is more interested in his feat with the ruler than in a possible client, but* Surtees *looks at him oddly.*)

Mr. Devizes. Surtees looks as if he thought you had.

(ROBERT *obliges by reflecting in the
light of* SURTEES'S *countenance.*)

ROBERT. Ah, you think it may have been
that one, Surty?

MR. DEVIZES (*sharply*). What one?

ROBERT. It was the day before yesterday.
You were out, father, and Surtees brought
me in some letters. His mouth was wide
open. (*Thoughtfully*) I suppose that was
why I did it.

MR. DEVIZES. What did you do?

ROBERT. I must have suddenly recalled a
game we used to play at Oxford. You
try to fling cards one by one into a hat.
It requires great skill. So I cast one
of the letters at Surtees's open mouth,
and it missed him and went into the fire.
It may have been Philip Ross's letter.

MR. DEVIZES (*wrinkling his brows*). Too bad,
Robert.

ROBERT (*blandly*). Yes, you see I am out of
practice.

SURTEES. He seemed a very nervous person,

sir, and quite young. Not a gentleman
of much consequence.

ROBERT (*airily*). Why not tell him to write
again?

MR. DEVIZES. Not fair.

SURTEES. But she——

ROBERT. She? Who?

SURTEES. There is a young lady with him,
sir. She is crying.

ROBERT. Pretty?

SURTEES. I should say she is pretty, sir, in
a quite inoffensive way.

ROBERT (*for his own gratification*). Ha!

MR. DEVIZES. Well, when I ring show them in.

ROBERT (*with roguish finger*). And let this
be a lesson to you, Surty, not to go about
your business with your mouth open.
(SURTEES *tries to smile as requested, but
with poor success.*) Nothing the matter,
Surty? You seem to have lost your
sense of humour.

SURTEES (*humbly enough*). I 'm afraid I have,
sir. I never had very much, Mr. Robert.

(*He goes quietly. There has been a
suppressed emotion about him that
makes the incident poignant.*)

ROBERT. Anything wrong with Surtees,
father?

MR. DEVIZES. Never mind him. I am very
angry with you, Robert.

ROBERT (*like one conceding a point in a de-
bating society*). And justly.

MR. DEVIZES (*frowning*). All we can do is
to tell this Mr. Ross that we have not
read his letter.

ROBERT (*bringing his knowledge of the world
to bear*). Is that necessary?

MR. DEVIZES. We must admit that we don't
know what he has come about.

ROBERT (*tolerant of his father's limitations*).
But don't we?

MR. DEVIZES. Do you?

ROBERT. I rather think I can put two and
two together.

MR. DEVIZES. Clever boy! Well, I shall
leave them to you.

Robert. Right.

Mr. Devizes. Your first case, Robert.

Robert (*undismayed*). It will be as good as a play to you to sit there and watch me discovering before they have been two minutes in the room what is the naughty thing that brings them here.

Mr. Devizes (*drily*). I am always ready to take a lesson from the new generation. But of course we old fogies could do that also.

Robert. How?

Mr. Devizes. By asking them.

Robert. Pooh. What did I go to Oxford for?

Mr. Devizes. God knows. Are you ready?

Robert. Quite.

(Mr. Devizes *rings*.)

Mr. Devizes. By the way, we don't know the lady's name.

Robert. Observe me finding it out.

Mr. Devizes. Is she married or single?

Robert. I 'll know at a glance. And mark

me, if she is married it is our nervous
gentleman who has come between her
and her husband; but if she is single it
is little Wet Face who has come between
him and his wife.

MR. DEVIZES. A Daniel!

    (*A young man and woman are shown
    in: very devoted to each other, though
    ROBERT does not know it. Yet it
    is the one thing obvious about them;
    more obvious than his cheap suit,
    which she presses so carefully beneath
    the mattress every night, or than the
    strength of his boyish face. Think-
    ing of him as he then was by the light
    of subsequent events one wonders
    whether if he had come alone some-
    thing disquieting could have been read
    in that face which was not there while
    she was by. Probably not; it was
    certainly already there, but had not yet
    reached the surface. With her, too,
    though she is to be what is called*

*changed before we see them again, all
seems serene; no warning signals; nothing in the way of their happiness in
each other but this alarming visit to
a lawyer's office. The stage direction might be 'Enter two lovers.'
He is scarcely the less nervous of the
two, but he enters stoutly in front of
her as if to receive the first charge.
She has probably nodded valiantly
to him outside the door, where she let
go his hand.)*

ROBERT (*master of the situation*). Come in,
Mr. Ross (*and he bows reassuringly to the
lady*). My partner—indeed my father.
(MR. DEVIZES *bows but remains in the
background.*)

PHILIP (*with a gulp*). You got my letter?

ROBERT. Yes—yes.

PHILIP. I gave you the details in it.

ROBERT. Yes, I have them all in my head.
(*Cleverly*) You will sit down, Miss— I
don't think I caught the name.

(*As much as to say, 'You see, father,
I spotted that she was single at
once.'*)

MR. DEVIZES (*who has also formed his opinion*).
You didn't ask for it, Robert.

ROBERT (*airily*). Miss—?

PHILIP. This is Mrs. Ross, my wife.

(ROBERT *is a little taken aback, and has
a conviction that his father is smiling.*)

ROBERT. Ah yes, of course; sit down,
please, Mrs. Ross.

(*She sits as if this made matters rather
worse.*)

PHILIP (*standing guard by her side*). My wife
is a little agitated.

ROBERT. Naturally. (*He tries a 'feeler.'*)
These affairs—very painful at the time—
but one gradually forgets.

EMILY (*with large eyes*). That is what Mr.
Ross says, but somehow I can't help—(*the
eyes fill*). You see, we have been married
only four months.

ROBERT. Ah—that does make it—yes, certainly. (*He becomes the wife's champion, and frowns on* PHILIP.)

PHILIP. I suppose the sum seems very small to you?

ROBERT (*serenely*). I confess that is the impression it makes on me.

PHILIP. I wish it was more.

ROBERT (*at a venture*). You are sure you can't make it more?

PHILIP. How can I?

ROBERT. Ha!

EMILY (*with sudden spirit*). I think it's a great deal.

PHILIP. Mrs. Ross is so nice about it.

ROBERT (*taking a strong line*). I think so. But she must not be taken advantage of. And of course we shall have something to say as to the amount.

PHILIP (*blankly*). In what way? There it is.

ROBERT (*guardedly*). Hum. Yes, in a sense.

EMILY (*breaking down*). Oh dear!

ROBERT (*more determined than ever to do his best for this wronged woman*). I am very

sorry, Mrs. Ross. (*Sternly*) I hope, sir,
you realise that the mere publicity to a
sensitive woman——

PHILIP. Publicity?

ROBERT (*feeling that he has got him on the
run*). Of course for her sake we shall
try to arrange things so that the names
do not appear. Still——

PHILIP. The names?

(*By this time* EMILY *is in tears.*)

EMILY. I can't help it. I love him so.

ROBERT (*still benighted*). Enough to forgive
him? (*Seeing himself suddenly as a media-
tor*) Mrs. Ross, is it too late to patch
things up?

PHILIP (*now in flame*). What do you mean,
sir?

MR. DEVIZES (*who has been quietly enjoying
himself*). Yes, Robert, what do you mean
precisely?

ROBERT. Really I—(*he tries brow-beating*)
I must tell you at once, Mr. Ross, that
unless a client gives us his fullest con-

fidence we cannot undertake a case of this kind.

PHILIP. A case of what kind, sir? If you are implying anything against my good name——

ROBERT. On your honour, sir, is there nothing against it?

PHILIP. I know of nothing, sir.

EMILY. Anything against my husband, Mr. Devizes! He is an angel.

ROBERT (*suddenly seeing that little Wet Face must be the culprit*). Then it is you.

EMILY. Oh, sir, what is me?

PHILIP. Answer that, sir.

ROBERT. Yes, Mr. Ross, I will. (*But he finds he cannot.*) On second thoughts I decline. I cannot believe it has been all this lady's fault, and I decline to have anything to do with such a painful case.

MR. DEVIZES (*promptly*). Then I will take it up.

PHILIP (*not to be placated*). I think your son has insulted me.

EMILY. Philip, come away.

MR. DEVIZES. One moment, please. As *1* did not see your letter, may I ask Mr. Ross what is your business with us?

PHILIP. I called to ask whether you would be so good as to draw up my will.

ROBERT (*blankly*). Your will! Is that all?

PHILIP. Certainly.

MR. DEVIZES. Now we know, Robert.

ROBERT. But Mrs. Ross's agitation?

PHILIP (*taking her hand*). She feels that to make my will brings my death nearer.

ROBERT. So that 's it.

PHILIP. It was all in the letter.

MR. DEVIZES (*coyly*). Anything to say, Robert?

ROBERT. Most—ah—extremely— (*He has an inspiration.*) But even now I 'm puzzled. You are Edgar Charles Ross?

PHILIP. No, Philip Ross.

ROBERT (*brazenly*). Philip Ross? We have made an odd mistake, father. (*There is a twinkle in* MR. DEVIZES'S *eye. He watches interestedly to see how his son is to emerge from the mess.*) The fact is, Mrs. Ross, we are expecting to-day a Mr. Edgar Charles Ross on a matter—well— of a kind— Ah me. (*With fitting gravity*) His wife, in short.

EMILY (*who has not read the newspapers in vain*). How awful. How sad.

ROBERT. Sad indeed. You will quite understand that professional etiquette prevents my saying one word more.

PHILIP. Yes, of course—we have no desire— But I did write.

ROBERT. Assuredly. But about a will. That is my father's department. No doubt you recall the letter now, father?

MR. DEVIZES (*who if he won't hinder won't help*). I can't say I do.

ROBERT (*unabashed*). Odd. You must have overlooked it.

MR. DEVIZES. Ha. At all events, Mr. Ross, I am quite at your service now.

PHILIP. Thank you.

ROBERT (*still ready to sacrifice himself on the call of duty*). You don't need me any more, father?

MR. DEVIZES. No, Robert; many thanks. You run off to your club now and have a bit of lunch. You must be tired. Send Surtees in to me. (*To his clients*) My son had his first case to-day.

PHILIP (*politely*). I hope successfully.

MR. DEVIZES. Not so bad. He rather bungled it at first, but he got out of a hole rather cleverly. I think you'll make a lawyer yet, Robert.

ROBERT. Thank you, father. (*He goes jauntily, with a flower in his button-hole.*)

MR. DEVIZES. Now, Mr. Ross.

> (*The young wife's hand goes out for comfort and finds* PHILIP'S *waiting for it.*)

PHILIP. What I want myself is that the will should all go into one sentence, 'I leave everything of which I die possessed to my beloved wife.'

MR. DEVIZES (*thawing to the romance of this young couple*). Well, there have been many worse wills than that, sir.

(EMILY *is emotional.*)

PHILIP. Don't give way, Emily.

EMILY. It was those words, 'of which I die possessed.' (*Imploringly*) Surely he doesn't need to say that—please, Mr. Devizes?

MR. DEVIZES. Certainly not. I am confident I can draw up the will without mentioning death at all.

EMILY (*huskily*). Oh, thank you.

MR. DEVIZES. At the same time, of course, in a legal document in which the widow is the sole——

(EMILY *again needs attention.*)

PHILIP (*reproachfully*). What was the need of saying 'widow'?

MR. DEVIZES. I beg your pardon, Mrs. Ross. I unreservedly withdraw the word 'widow.' Forgive a stupid old solicitor. (*She smiles gratefully through her tears.*

SURTEES *comes in*.) Surtees, just take a few notes, please. (SURTEES *sits in the background and takes notes*.) The facts of the case, as I understand, Mrs. Ross, are these: Your husband (*Quickly*)—who is in the prime of health—but knows life to be uncertain——

EMILY. Oh!

MR. DEVIZES. —though usually, as we learn from holy script itself, it lasts seven times ten years—and believing that he will in all probability live the allotted span, nevertheless, because of his love of you thinks it judicious to go through the form—it is a mere form—of making a will.

EMILY (*fervently*). Oh, thank you.

MR. DEVIZES. Any details, Mr. Ross?

PHILIP. I am an orphan. I live at Belvedere, 14 Tulphin Road, Hammersmith.

EMILY (*to whom the address has a seductive sound*). We live there.

PHILIP. And I am a clerk in the employ of

Curar and Gow, the foreign coaling agents.

MR. DEVIZES. Yes, yes. Any private income?

(*They cannot help sniggering a little at the quaint question.*)

PHILIP. Oh no!

MR. DEVIZES. I see it will be quite a brief will.

PHILIP (*to whom the remark sounds scarcely worthy of a great occasion*). My income is a biggish one.

MR. DEVIZES. Yes?

EMILY (*important*). He has £170 a year.

MR. DEVIZES. Ah.

PHILIP. I began at £60. But it is going up, Mr. Devizes, by leaps and bounds. Another £15 this year.

MR. DEVIZES. Good.

PHILIP (*darkly*). I have a certain ambition.

EMILY (*eagerly*). Tell him, Philip.

PHILIP (*with a big breath*). We have made up our minds to come to £365 a year before I—retire.

EMILY. That is a pound a day.

MR. DEVIZES (*smiling sympathetically on them*). So it is. My best wishes.

PHILIP. Thank you. Of course the furnishing took a good deal.

MR. DEVIZES. It would.

EMILY. He insisted on my having the very best. (*She ceases. She is probably thinking of her superb spare bedroom.*)

PHILIP. But we are not a penny in debt; and I have £200 saved.

MR. DEVIZES. I think you have made a brave beginning.

EMILY. They have the highest opinion of him in the office.

PHILIP. Then I am insured for £500.

MR. DEVIZES. I am glad to hear that.

PHILIP. Of course I would like to leave her a house in Kensington and a carriage and pair.

MR. DEVIZES. Who knows, perhaps you will.

EMILY. Oh!

MR. DEVIZES. Forgive me.

Emily. What would houses and horses be to me without him!

Mr. Devizes (*soothingly*). Quite so. What I take Mr. Ross to mean is that when he dies—if he ever should die—everything is to go to his—his spouse.

Philip (*dogged*). Yes.

Emily (*dogged*). No.

Philip (*sighing*). This is the only difference we have ever had. Mrs. Ross insists on certain bequests. You see, I have two cousins, ladies, not well off, whom I have been in the way of helping a little. But in my will, how can I?

Mr. Devizes. You must think first of your wife.

Philip. But she insists on my leaving £50 to each of them. (*He looks appealingly to his wife.*)

Emily (*grandly*). £100.

Philip. £50.

Emily. Dear, £100.

Mr. Devizes. Let us say £75.

PHILIP (*reluctantly*). Very well.

EMILY. No, £100.

PHILIP. She 'll have to get her way. Here
are their names and addresses.

MR. DEVIZES. Anything else?

PHILIP (*hurriedly*). No.

EMILY. The convalescent home, dear. He was
in it a year ago, and they were so kind.

PHILIP. Yes, but——

EMILY. £10. (*He has to yield, with a reproachful, admiring look.*)

MR. DEVIZES. Then if that is all, I won't detain you. If you look in to-morrow, Mr.
Ross, about this time, we shall have
everything ready for you.

(*Their faces fall.*)

EMILY. Oh, Mr. Devizes, if only it could all
be drawn up now, and done with.

PHILIP. You see, sir, we are screwed up to it
to-day.

(*'Our fate is in your hands,' they might
be saying, and the lawyer smiles to
find himself such a power.*)

Mr. Devizes (*looking at his watch*). Well, it certainly need not take long. You go out and have lunch somewhere, and then come back.

Emily. Oh, don't ask me to eat.

Philip. We are too excited.

Emily. Please may we just walk about the street?

Mr. Devizes (*smiling*). Of course you may, you ridiculous young wife.

Emily. I know it's ridiculous of me, but I am so fond of him.

Mr. Devizes. Yes, it is ridiculous. But don't change; especially if you get on in the world, Mr. Ross.

Philip. No fear!

Emily (*backing from the will, which may now be said to be in existence*). And please don't give us a copy of it to keep. I would rather not have it in the house.

Mr. Devizes (*nodding reassuringly*). In an hour's time. (*They go, and the lawyer has his lunch, which is simpler than*

ROBERT'S: *a sandwich and a glass of wine.
He speaks as he eats.*) You will get that
ready, Surtees. Here are the names and
addresses he left. (*Cheerily*) A nice
couple.

SURTEES (*who is hearing another voice*). Yes,
sir.

MR. DEVIZES (*unbending*). Little romance of
its kind. Makes one feel quite gay.

SURTEES. Yes, sir.

MR. DEVIZES (*struck perhaps by the deadness
of his voice*). You don't look very gay,
Surtees.

SURTEES. I'm sorry, sir. We can't all be
gay. (*He is going out without looking at
his employer.*) I'll see to this, sir.

MR. DEVIZES. Stop a minute. Is there anything wrong? (SURTEES *has difficulty
in answering, and* MR. DEVIZES *goes to
him kindly.*) Not worrying over that
matter we spoke about? (SURTEES *in-
clines his head.*) Is the pain worse?

SURTEES. It's no great pain, sir.

MR. DEVIZES (*uncomfortably*). I 'm sure it 's
 not—what you fear. Any specialist
 would tell you so.

SURTEES (*without looking up*). I have been
 to one, sir—yesterday.

MR. DEVIZES. Well?

SURTEES. It 's—that, sir.

MR. DEVIZES. He couldn't be sure.

SURTEES. Yes, sir.

MR. DEVIZES. An operation——

SURTEES. Too late, he said, for that. If I
 had been operated on long ago there
 might have been a chance.

MR. DEVIZES. But you didn't have it long ago.

SURTEES. Not to my knowledge, sir; but
 he says it was there all the same, always
 in me, a black spot, not so big as a pin's
 head, but waiting to spread and destroy
 me in the fulness of time. All the rest
 of me as sound as a bell. (*That is the
 voice that* SURTEES *has been hearing.*)

MR. DEVIZES (*helpless*). It seems damnably
 unfair.

Surtees (*humbly*). I don't know, sir. He says there's a spot of that kind in pretty nigh all of us, and if we don't look out it does for us in the end.

Mr. Devizes (*hurriedly*). No, no, no.

Surtees. He called it the accursed thing. I think he meant we should know of it and be on the watch. (*He pulls himself together.*) I'll see to this at once, sir.

(*He goes out. Mr. Devizes continues his lunch.*)

The curtain falls here for a moment only, to indicate the passing of a number of years. When it rises we see that the engraving of Queen Victoria has given way to one of King Edward.

Robert *is discovered, immersed in affairs. He is now a middle-aged man who has long forgotten how to fling cards into a hat. To him comes* Sennet, *a brisk clerk.*

SENNET. Mrs. Philip Ross to see you, sir.

ROBERT. Mr. Ross, don't you mean, Sennet?

SENNET. No, sir.

ROBERT. Ha. It was Mr. Ross I was expecting. Show her in. (*Frowning*) And, Sennet, less row in the office, if you please.

SENNET (*glibly*). It was these young clerks, sir——

ROBERT. They mustn't be young here, or they go. Tell them that.

SENNET (*glad to be gone*). Yes, sir.

(*He shows in* MRS. ROSS. *We have not seen her for twenty years and would certainly not recognise her in the street. So shrinking her first entrance into this room, but she sails in now like a galleon. She is not so much dressed as richly upholstered. She is very sure of herself. Yet she is not a different woman from the* EMILY *we remember; the pity of it is that somehow this is the same woman.*)

ROBERT (*who makes much of his important visitor and is also wondering why she has come*). This is a delightful surprise, Mrs. Ross. Allow me. (*He removes her fine cloak with proper solicitude, and* EMILY *walks out of it in the manner that makes it worth possessing.*) This chair, alas, is the best I can offer you.

EMILY (*who is still a good-natured woman if you attempt no nonsense with her*). It will do quite well.

ROBERT (*gallantly*). Honoured to see you in it.

EMILY (*smartly*). Not you. You were saying to yourself, 'Now, what brings the woman here?'

ROBERT. Honestly, I——

EMILY. And I'll tell you. You are expecting Mr. Ross, I think?

ROBERT (*cautiously*). Well—ah——

EMILY. Pooh. The cunning of you lawyers. I know he has an appointment with you, and that is why I've come.

ROBERT. He arranged with you to meet him here?

EMILY (*preening herself*). I wouldn't say that. I don't know that he will be specially pleased to find me here when he comes.

ROBERT (*guardedly*). Oh?

EMILY (*who is now a woman that goes straight to her goal*). I know what he is coming about. To make a new will.

ROBERT (*admitting it*). After all, not the first he has made with us, Mrs. Ross.

EMILY (*promptly*). No, the fourth.

ROBERT (*warming his hands at the thought*). Such a wonderful career. He goes from success to success.

EMILY (*complacently*). Yes, we 're big folk.

ROBERT. You are indeed.

EMILY (*sharply*). But the last will covered everything.

ROBERT (*on guard again*). Of course it is a matter I cannot well discuss even with you. And I know nothing of his intentions.

EMILY. Well, I suspect some of them.

ROBERT. Ah.

EMILY. And that's why I'm here. Just to see that he does nothing foolish.

> (*She settles herself more comfortably as* MR. ROSS *is announced. A city magnate walks in. You know he is that before you see that he is* PHILIP ROSS.)

PHILIP (*speaking as he enters*). How do, Devizes, how do. Well, let us get at this thing at once. Time is money, you know, time is money. (*Then he sees his wife.*) Hello, Emily.

EMILY (*unperturbed*). You didn't ask me to come, Philip, but I thought I might as well.

PHILIP. That's all right.

> (*His brow had lowered at first sight of her, but now he gives her cleverness a grin of respect.*)

EMILY. It is the first will you have made

without taking me into your confidence.

PHILIP. No important changes. I just thought to save you the—unpleasantness of the thing.

EMILY. How do you mean?

PHILIP (*fidgeting*). Well, one can't draw up a will without feeling for the moment that he is bringing his end nearer. Is that not so, Devizes?

ROBERT (*who will quite possibly die intestate*). Some do have that feeling.

EMILY. But what nonsense. How can it have any effect of that kind one way or the other?

ROBERT. Quite so.

EMILY (*reprovingly*). Just silly sentiment, Philip. I would have thought it would be a pleasure to you handling such a big sum.

PHILIP (*wincing*). Not handling it, giving it up.

EMILY. To those you love.

PHILIP (*rather shortly*). I 'm not giving it up yet. You talk as if I was on my last legs.

EMILY (*imperturbably*). Not at all. It 's you that are doing that.

ROBERT (*to the rescue*). Here is my copy of the last will. I don't know if you would like me to read it out?

PHILIP. It 's hardly necessary.

EMILY. We have our own copy at home and we know it well.

PHILIP (*sitting back in his chair*). What do you think I 'm worth to-day, Devizes?

(*Every one smiles. It is as if the sun had peeped in at the window.*)

ROBERT. I daren't guess.

PHILIP. An easy seventy thou.

EMILY. And that 's not counting the house and the country cottage. We call it a cottage. You should see it!

ROBERT. I have heard of it.

EMILY (*more sharply, though the sun still shines*). Well, go on, Philip. I suppose

you are not thinking of cutting me out
of anything.

PHILIP (*heartily*). Of course not. There will
be more to you than ever.

EMILY (*coolly*). There's more to leave.

PHILIP (*hesitating*). At the same time——

EMILY. Well? It's to be mine absolutely
of course. Not just a life interest.

PHILIP (*doggedly*). That is a change I was
thinking of.

EMILY. Just what I have suspected for days.
Will you please to say why?

ROBERT (*whose client after all is the man*). Of
course it is quite common.

EMILY. I didn't think my husband was quite
common.

ROBERT. I only mean that as there are
children——

PHILIP. That's what I mean too.

EMILY. And I can't be trusted to leave my
money to my own children! In what
way have I ever failed them before?

PHILIP (*believing it too*). Never, Emily, never.

A more devoted mother— If you have
one failing it is that you spoil them.

EMILY. Then what's your reason?

PHILIP (*less sincerely*). Just to save you
worry when I'm gone.

EMILY. It's no worry to me to look after
my money.

PHILIP (*bridling*). After all, it's my money.

EMILY. I knew that was what was at the
back of your mind.

PHILIP (*reverently*). It's such a great
sum.

EMILY. One would think you were afraid I
would marry again.

PHILIP (*snapping*). One would think you
looked to my dying next week.

EMILY. Tuts.

(PHILIP *is unable to sit still.*)

PHILIP. My money. If you were to invest
it badly and lose it. I tell you, Devizes,
I couldn't lie quiet in my grave if I
thought my money was lost by injudicious
investments.

EMILY (*coldly*). You are thinking of yourself, Philip, rather than of the children.

PHILIP. Not at all.

ROBERT (*hastily*). How are the two children?

EMILY. Though I say it myself, there never were better. Harry is at Eton, you know, the most fashionable school in the country.

ROBERT. Doing well, I hope.

PHILIP (*chuckling*). We have the most gratifying letters from him. Last Saturday he was caught smoking cigarettes with a lord. (*With pardonable pride*) They were sick together.

ROBERT. And Miss Gwendolen? She must be almost grown up now.

> (*The parents exchange important glances.*)

EMILY. Should we tell him?

PHILIP. Under the rose, you know, Devizes.

ROBERT. Am I to congratulate her?

EMILY. No names, Philip.

PHILIP. No, no names—but she won't be a plain Mrs., no sir.

ROBERT. Well done, Miss Gwendolen. (*With fitting jocularity*) Now I see why you want a new will.

PHILIP. Yes, that's my main reason, Emily.

EMILY. But none of your life interests for me, Philip.

PHILIP (*shying*). We'll talk that over presently.

ROBERT. Will you keep the legacies as they are?

PHILIP. Well, there's that £500 for the hospitals.

EMILY. Yes, with so many claims on us, is that necessary?

PHILIP (*becoming stouter*). I'm going to make it £1000.

EMILY. Philip!

PHILIP. My mind is made up. I want to make a splash with the hospitals.

ROBERT (*hurrying to the next item*). There is £50 a year each to two cousins, ladies.

PHILIP. I suppose we'll keep that as it is, Emily?

EMILY. It was just gifts to them of £100 each at first.

PHILIP. I was poor at that time myself.

EMILY. Do you think it's wise to load them with so much money? They'll not know what to do with it.

PHILIP. They're old.

EMILY. But they're wiry. £75 a year between them would surely be enough.

PHILIP. It would be if they lived together, but you see they don't. They hate each other like cat and dog.

EMILY. That's not nice between relatives. You could leave it to them on condition that they do live together. That would be a Christian action.

PHILIP. There's something in that.

ROBERT. Then the chief matter is whether Mrs. Ross——

EMILY. Oh, I thought that was settled.

PHILIP (*with a sigh*). I'll have to give in to her, sir.

ROBERT. Very well. I suppose my father

will want to draw up the will. I'm
sorry he had to be in the country to-day.

EMILY (*affable now that she has gained her
point*). I hope he is wearing well?

ROBERT. Wonderfully. He is away playing
golf.

PHILIP (*grinning*). Golf. I have no time
for games. (*Considerately*) But he must
get the drawing up of my will. I couldn't
deprive the old man of that.

ROBERT. He will be proud to do it again.

PHILIP (*well satisfied*). Ah! There's many
a one would like to look over your father's
shoulder when he's drawing up my will.
I wonder what I'll cut up for in the end.
But I must be going.

EMILY. Can I drop you anywhere? I have
the greys out.

PHILIP. Yes, at the club.

    (*Now* MRS. ROSS *walks into her cloak.*)
Good-day, Devizes. I won't have time
to look in again, so tell the old man to
come to me.

ROBERT (*deferentially*). Whatever suits you
best. (*Ringing.*) He will be delighted.
I remember his saying to me on the day
you made your first will——

PHILIP (*chuckling*). A poor little affair that.

ROBERT. He said to me you were a couple
whose life looked like being a romance.

PHILIP. And he was right—eh, Emily?—
though he little thought what a romance.

EMILY. No, he little thought what a romance.

> (*They make a happy departure, and
> ROBERT is left reflecting.*)

*The curtain again falls, and rises im-
mediately, as the engraving shows,
on the same office in the reign of King
George. It is a foggy morning and
a fire burns briskly. MR. DEVIZES,
SENIOR, arrives for the day's work
just as he came daily for over half
a century. But he has no right to
be here now. A year or two ago
they got him to retire, as he was grown*

*feeble; and there is an understanding
that he does not go out of his house
alone. He has, as it were, escaped
to-day, and his feet have carried him
to the old office that is the home of
his mind. He was almost portly
when we saw him first, but he has
become little again and as light as the
schoolboy whose deeds are nearer to
him than many of the events of later
years. He arrives at the office,
thinking it is old times, and a clerk surveys him uncomfortably from the door.*

CREED (*not quite knowing what to do*). Mr.
Devizes has not come in yet, sir.

MR. DEVIZES (*considering*). Yes, I have.
Do you mean Mr. Robert?

CREED. Yes, sir.

MR. DEVIZES (*querulously*). Always late.
Can't get that boy to settle down.
(*Leniently*) Well, well, boys will be
boys—eh, Surtees?

CREED (*wishing* MR. ROBERT *would come*). My name is Creed, sir.

MR. DEVIZES (*sharply*). Creed? Don't know you. Where is Surtees?

CREED. There is no one of that name in the office, sir.

MR. DEVIZES (*growing timid*). No? I re-member now. Poor Surtees! (*But his mind cannot grapple with troubles.*) Tell him I want him when he comes in.

> (*He is changing, after his old custom, into an office coat.*)

CREED. That is Mr. Dev—Mr. Robert's coat, sir.

MR. DEVIZES. He has no business to hang it there. That is my nail.

CREED. He has hung it there for years, sir.

MR. DEVIZES. Not at all. I must have it. Why does Surtees let him do it? Help me into my office coat, boy.

> (CREED *helps him into the coat he has taken off, and the old man is content.*)

CREED (*seeing him lift up the correspondence*).
I don't think Mr. Devizes would like you
to open the office letters, sir.

MR. DEVIZES (*pettishly*). What's that? Go
away, boy.   Send Surtees.

> (*To the relief of* CREED, ROBERT *arrives,
> and, taking in the situation, signs to
> the clerk to go.   He has a more youth-
> ful manner than when last we saw him,
> has* ROBERT, *but his hair is iron grey.
> He is kindly to his father.*)

ROBERT. You here, father?

MR. DEVIZES (*after staring at him*). Yes, you
are Robert. (*A little frightened.*) You
are an old man, Robert.

ROBERT (*without wincing*). Getting on, father.
But why did they let you come? You
haven't been here for years.

MR. DEVIZES (*puzzled*). Years? I think I
just came in the old way, Robert, without
thinking.

ROBERT. Yes, yes.   I 'll get some one to go
home with you.

MR. DEVIZES (*rather abject*). Let me stay, Robert. I like being here. I won't disturb you. I like the smell of the office, Robert.

ROBERT. Of course you may stay. Come over to the fire. (*He settles his father by the fire in the one arm-chair.*) There; you can have a doze by the fire.

MR. DEVIZES. A doze by the fire. That is all I'm good for now. Once—but my son hangs his coat there now. (*Presently he looks up fearfully.*) Robert, tell me something in a whisper: Is Surtees dead?

ROBERT (*who has forgotten the name*). Surtees?

MR. DEVIZES. My clerk, you know.

ROBERT. Oh. Why, he has been dead this thirty years, father.

MR. DEVIZES. So long! Seems like yesterday.

ROBERT. It is just far back times that seem clear to you now.

MR. DEVIZES (*meekly*). Is it.

(ROBERT *opens his letters, and his*
father falls asleep. CREED *comes.*)

CREED. Sir Philip Ross.

(*The great* SIR PHILIP *enters, nearly*
sixty now, strong of frame still, but
a lost man. He is in mourning,
and carries the broken pieces of his
life with an air of braggadocio.
It should be understood that he is not
a 'sympathetic' part, and any actor
who plays him as such will be rolling
the play in the gutter.)

ROBERT (*on his feet at once to greet such a*
client). You, Sir Philip.

PHILIP (*head erect*). Here I am.

ROBERT (*because it will out*). How are
you?

PHILIP (*as if challenged*). I'm all right—
great. (*With defiant jocularity*) Called on
the old business.

ROBERT. To make another will?

PHILIP. You've guessed it—the very first
time. (*He sees the figure by the fire.*)

Robert. Yes, it's my father. He's dozing. Shouldn't be here at all. He forgets things. It's just age.

Philip (*grimly*). Forgets things. That must be fine.

Robert (*conventionally*). I should like, Sir Philip, to offer you my sincere condolences. In the midst of life we are— How true that is. I attended the funeral.

Philip. I saw you.

Robert. A much esteemed lady. I had a great respect for her.

Philip (*almost with relish*). Do you mind, when we used to come here about the will, somehow she—we—always took for granted I should be the first to go.

Robert (*devoutly*). These things are hid from mortal eyes.

Philip (*with conviction*). There's a lot hid. We needn't have worried so much about the will if—well, let us get at it. (*Fiercely*) I haven't given in, you know.

Robert. We must bow our heads——

PHILIP. Must we?   Am I bowing mine?

ROBERT (*uncomfortably*). Such courage in the great hour—yes—and I am sure Lady Ross——

PHILIP (*with the ugly humour that has come to him*). She wasn't that.

ROBERT. The honour came so soon afterwards—I feel she would like to be thought of as Lady Ross. I shall always remember her as a fine lady richly dressed who used——

PHILIP (*harshly*). Stop it.   That's not how I think of her.   There was a time before that—she wasn't richly dressed—(*he stamps upon his memories*).   Things went wrong, I don't know how.   It's a beast of a world.   I didn't come here to talk about that.   Let us get to work.

ROBERT (*turning with relief from the cemetery*). Yes, yes, and after all life has its compensations.   You have your son who——

PHILIP (*snapping*). No, I haven't. (*This startles the lawyer.*)   I'm done with him.

ROBERT. If he has been foolish——

PHILIP. Foolish! (*Some dignity comes into the man.*) Sir, I have come to a pass when foolish as applied to my own son would seem to me a very pretty word.

ROBERT. Is it as bad as that?

PHILIP. He's a rotter.

ROBERT. It is very painful to me to hear you say that.

PHILIP. More painful, think you, than for me to say it? (*Clenching his fists.*) But I've shipped him off. The law had to wink at it, or I couldn't have done it. Why don't you say I pampered him and it serves me right? It's what they are all saying behind my back. Why don't you ask me about my girl? That's another way to rub it in.

ROBERT. Don't, Sir Philip. I knew her. My sympathy——

PHILIP. A chauffeur, that is what he was. The man who drove her own car.

ROBERT. I was deeply concerned——

PHILIP. I want nobody's pity. I 've done with both of them, and if you think I 'm a broken man you 're much mistaken. I 'll show them. Have you your papers there? Then take down my last will. I have everything in my head. I 'll show them.

ROBERT. Would it not be better to wait till a calmer——

PHILIP. Will you do it now, or am I to go across the street?

ROBERT. If I must.

PHILIP. Then down with it. (*He wets his lips.*) I, Philip Ross, of 77 Bath Street, W., do hereby revoke all former wills and testaments, and I leave everything of which I die possessed——

ROBERT. Yes?

PHILIP. Everything of which I die possessed——

ROBERT. Yes?

PHILIP. I leave it—I leave it— (*The game is up.*) My God, Devizes, I don't know what to do with it.

ROBERT. I—I—really—come——

PHILIP (*cynically*). Can't you make any sug-
gestions?

ROBERT. Those cousins are dead, I think?

PHILIP. Years ago.

ROBERT (*troubled*). In the case of such a
large sum——

PHILIP (*letting all his hoarded gold run through
his fingers*). The money I've won with
my blood. God in heaven! (*Showing his
teeth.*) Would that old man like it to
play with? If I bring it to you in
sacks, will you fling it out of the window
for me?

ROBERT. Sir Philip!

PHILIP (*taking a paper from his pocket*). Here,
take this. It has the names and addresses of the half-dozen men I've fought
with most for gold; and I've beaten
them. Draw up a will leaving all my
money to be divided between them, with
my respectful curses, and bring it to my
house and I'll sign it.

ROBERT (*properly shocked*). But really I can't possibly——

PHILIP. Either you or another; is it to be you?

ROBERT. Very well.

PHILIP. Then that's settled. (*He rises with a laugh. He regards* MR. DEVIZES *quizzically.*) So you weren't in at the last will after all, old Sleep by the Fire.

(*To their surprise the old man stirs.*)

MR. DEVIZES. What's that about a will?

ROBERT. You are awake, father?

MR. DEVIZES (*whose eyes have opened on* PHILIP's *face*). I don't know you, sir.

ROBERT. Yes, yes, father, you remember Mr. Ross. He is Sir Philip now.

MR. DEVIZES (*courteously*). Sir Philip? I wish you joy, sir, but I don't know you.

ROBERT (*encouragingly*). Ross, father.

MR. DEVIZES. I knew a Mr. Ross long ago.

ROBERT. This is the same.

MR. DEVIZES (*annoyed*). No, no. A bright young fellow he was, with such a dear.

Children of Thrums Try Not to Be "Muckle Sad" as Fairy Godfather Of Childhood Is Laid to His Rest

[Canadian Press Cable]

KIRRIEMUIR, Forfarshire, Scotland, June 24. — Sir James Barrie, the creator of Peter Pan, was buried today in this little weaving village—the "Thrums" of his Scottish tales—where he was born 77 years ago.

At the village gates 300 children, who had been taught to regard Sir James as the fairy godfather of all children, met the coffin. Also there was 87-year-old Alexander Lowson, schoolmate and lifelong friend of Barrie, who said sadly:

"Puir Jimmy. This is a sad day for Thrums, but I know he would'na want us to be muckle sad."

The famous author, who died last Saturday in a London nursing home of bronchial pneumonia, was buried in the family plot in the Hillside cemetery after services at St. Mary's Anglican church. The pallbearers were all Kirriemuir people who were intimately acquainted with their famous townsman.

There were a few visiting notables, but most of those attending the funeral were simple folk who loved Barrie in their simple way. All hotels in the district were filled overnight and many sought accommodation in the red stone homes of the village.

Pan Pipes a Dirge

PAN'S pipes sound sadly today in Kensington Gardens, London, as Sir James Barrie is laid to rest in his native Kirriemuir.

pretty wife. They came to make a will.
(*He chuckles.*) And bless me, they had
only twopence halfpenny. I took a
fancy to them; such a happy pair.

ROBERT (*apologetically*). The past is clearer
to him than the present nowadays. That
will do, father.

PHILIP (*brusquely*). Let him go on.

MR. DEVIZES. Poor souls, it all ended un-
happily, you know.

PHILIP (*who is not brusque to him*). Yes, I
know. Why did things go wrong, sir?
I sit and wonder, and I can't find the
beginning.

MR. DEVIZES. That's the sad part of it.
There was never a beginning. It was
always there. He told me all about it.

ROBERT. He is thinking of something else;
I don't know what.

PHILIP. Quiet. What was it that was
always there?

MR. DEVIZES. It was always in them—a spot
no bigger than a pin's head, but waiting

to spread and destroy them in the fulness
of time.

ROBERT. I don't know what he has got hold
of.

PHILIP. He knows. Could they have done
anything to prevent it, sir?

MR. DEVIZES. If they had been on the watch.
But they didn't know, so they weren't
on the watch. Poor souls.

PHILIP. Poor souls.

MR. DEVIZES. It's called the accursed thing.
It gets nearly everybody in the end, if
they don't look out.

> (*He sinks back into his chair and
> forgets them.*)

ROBERT. He is just wandering.

PHILIP. The old man knows.

> (*He slowly tears up the paper he had
> given* ROBERT.)

ROBERT (*relieved*). I am glad to see you do
that.

PHILIP. A spot no bigger than a pin's head.

> (*A wish wells up in him, too late perhaps.*)

I wish I could help some young things before that spot has time to spread and destroy them as it has destroyed me and mine.

ROBERT (*brightly*). With such a large fortune——

PHILIP (*summing up his life*). It can't be done with money, sir.

(*He goes away; God knows where.*)

DER TAG

A PLAY

DER TAG

A bare chamber lighted by a penny dip which casts shadows. On a hard chair by a table sits an EMPEROR *in thought. To him come his* CHANCELLOR *and an* OFFICER.

CHANCELLOR. Your Imperial Majesty——
OFFICER. Sire——
> (*The* EMPEROR *rises.*)
EMPEROR. Is that the paper?
> (*Indicating paper in* CHANCELLOR'S
> *hand.*)
CHANCELLOR (*giving it to him*). It awaits only your Imperial Majesty's signature.
OFFICER. When you have signed that paper, sire, the Fatherland will be at war with France and Russia.
EMPEROR. At last! This little paper——
CHANCELLOR. Not of the value of a bird's

feather until it has your royal signature.
Then——

EMPEROR. Then it will sing round the planet,
the vibration of it will not pass in a hundred years. My friend, how still the
world has grown since I raised this pen.
All Europe's listening. Europe! That's
Germany, when I have signed. And
yet——

OFFICER. Your Imperial Majesty is not
afraid to sign?

EMPEROR (*flashing*). Afraid!

OFFICER (*abject*). Oh, sire!

EMPEROR. I am irresistible to-day! "Red
blood boils in my veins, to me every
open door is the gift of a world, I hear
a thousand nightingales, I could eat
all the elephants in Hindustan and pick
my teeth with the spire of Strasburg
Cathedral."

OFFICER. That is the Fatherland to-day.
Such as we are, that you have made us,
each seeking to copy you in so far as man

can repeat his deity. It was you fashioned us into a sword, sire, and now the sword must speak.

EMPEROR (*approvingly*). There the sword spoke. And yet the wise one said: "Take not your enemies together but separately, lest the meal go to them instead of to you." One at a time! (*To* CHANCELLOR) Why am I not a friend of Russia till France is out of the way, or France's friend until the Bear is muzzled? That was your part.

CHANCELLOR. For that I strove, but their mean minds suspected me. Sire, your signature?

EMPEROR. What of Britain?

OFFICER (*intently*). This. THE DAY, to which we have so often drunk, draws near.

EMPEROR. The Day! To The Day! (*All salute The Day with their swords.*) But when?

OFFICER. Now if she wants it.

EMPEROR. There is no road to Britain— until our neighbours are subdued. Then, for us, there will be no roads that do not lead to Britain.

CHANCELLOR (*suavely*). Your Imperial Majesty, Britain will not join in just now.

EMPEROR. If I was sure of that?

CHANCELLOR. I vouch for it. So well we've chosen our time, it finds her at issue with herself, her wild women let loose, her colonies ready to turn against her, Ireland aflame, her paltry British Army sulking with the civic powers.

EMPEROR. These wounds might heal suddenly if German bugles sounded. It is a land that in the past has done things.

OFFICER. In the past, your Imperial Majesty; but in the past alone lies Britain's greatness.

EMPEROR. Yes, that's the German truth. Britain has grown dull and sluggish; a belly of a land, she lies overfed, no dreams within her such as keep Powers alive; and timid, too—without red blood in her, but in its stead a thick yellowish fluid. The

most she'll play for is her own safety;
pretend to grant her that, and she'll seek
her soft bed again.   Britain's part in the
world's making is done: "I was," her
epitaph.

CHANCELLOR. How well you know her, sire.
All she needs is some small excuse for saying: "I acted in the best interests of my
money-bags."   That excuse I've found for
her.   *I* have promised in your name a
secret compact with her that if she stands
aloof, the parts of France we do not
at present need we will not at present
take.

EMPEROR. A secret bargain over the head of
France, her friend!   Surely an infamous
proposal.

CHANCELLOR. The British Government will
not think so.   Trust me to know them,
sire.   Your signature?

EMPEROR (*gleaming*). I can fling a million
men within the week across the border by
way of Alsace and Lorraine.

OFFICER (*frowning*). There are a hundred gates to open that way.

EMPEROR. My guns shall open them.

OFFICER (*with meaning*). You can think of no easier road, sire?

EMPEROR. I think of it night and day.

OFFICER. One further north—through Belgium?

EMPEROR. If I could dare! But no, that road is barred.

OFFICER (*misunderstanding*). On the contrary, sire——

EMPEROR. Barred by a fortress no gun of mine may bear against—by honour, by our plighted word.

OFFICER. Yes, sire——

EMPEROR (*after hesitating*). No, no! I will not so stain my name.

CHANCELLOR. I am with you, sire, but I fear it will not be so with France. She has grown cynical. She will find the road through Belgium.

EMPEROR. You seek to tempt me. She also signed the treaty.

CHANCELLOR. Your Imperial Majesty judges others by yourself. I have private ground for fearing that in the greed for a first advantage, France will call the treaty but a scrap of paper.

EMPEROR. I think your private ground may be your own private newspaper.

CHANCELLOR. She will say that necessity knows no law, or some such dastard words.

EMPEROR. Belgium is no craven: she will fight the betrayer.

CHANCELLOR. France will hack her way through.

EMPEROR. My Chancellor, that is a hideous phrase.

CHANCELLOR. I ask your pardon, sire. It came, somehow, pat to my lips.

OFFICER. Your Imperial Majesty, the time passes—will it please you to sign?

CHANCELLOR. Buonaparte would have acted quickly.

EMPEROR. Buonaparte!

CHANCELLOR. The paper, sire.

EMPEROR. Leave it now with me. Return in an hour and you shall have it signed.

OFFICER (*warningly*). The least delay——

CHANCELLOR. Over-much reflection——

EMPEROR. I wish to be alone.

(*They retire respectfully, but anxious. He is left alone in thought.*)

EMPEROR. Even a King's life is but a day, and in his day the sun is only at its zenith once. This is my zenith; others will come to Germany, but not to me. The world pivots on me to-night. They said Buonaparte! coupling me with him. To dim Napoleon! Paris in three weeks— say four to cover any chance miscalculation. Russia on her back in six, with Poland snapping at her; and then after a breathing space we reach—The Day! We sweep the English Channel, changing its name as we embark, and cross by way of Calais, which will have fallen easily into our hands. The British Fleet destroyed—for that is part of the plan,— Dover to London is a week of leisured marching, and London itself, unfortified and panic-stricken, falls in a day. Væ Victis! I'll leave conquered Britain some balls to play with, so that there shall be no uprising. Next I carve America in great mouthfuls for my colonists, for now I stride the seas. It's all so docketed I feel it's as good as done before I set forth to do it. Dictator of the World! And all for pacific ends, for once the whole is mine we come at last to the great desideratum, a universal peace. Rulers over all! God in the heavens, I upon the earth—we two! (*Raising his eyes threateningly*) And there are still the Zeppelins! I'll sign.

> (*The* Spirit of Culture *appears—a noble female figure in white robes.*)

EMPEROR. Who's that?

CULTURE. A friend. I am Culture, who has so long hovered, well-pleased, over happy Germany.

EMPEROR (*who gives her royal honour*). A friend indeed—a consort! I would hear you say, O Queen, that I have done some things for you.

CULTURE. You have done much for me. I have held my head higher since you were added to the roll of Sovereigns. I may have smiled at you at times, as when you seemed to think that you were the two of us in one; but as Kings go, you have been a worthy King.

EMPEROR. It was all done for you.

CULTURE. So for long I thought. I looked upon Germany's golden granaries, plucked from ground once barren, its busy mills and furnaces, its outstretching commerce and teeming peoples and noble seats of learning, all mellowing in the sun; and I heard you say they were dedicated to me, and I was proud. You have honoured me, my Emperor, and now I am here to be abased by you. All the sweet garments you have robed me in—tear them off me, and send me naked out of Germany.

EMPEROR. You would not have me sign?

CULTURE. I warn you first to know yourself, you who have gloated in a looking-glass too long.

EMPEROR. I sign that Germany may be greater still. To spread your banner farther: thus I make the whole world cultured.

CULTURE. My banner needs no such spreading. It has ever been your weakness to think that I have no other home save here in Germany. I have many homes, and the fairest is in France.

EMPEROR. If that were true, Germany would care less for you.

CULTURE. If that is true, I have never had a home in Germany. I am no single nation's servant, no single race's queen. I am not of German make. My banner is already in every land on which you would place your heel. I'll not have you say it is for me you fight. Find some other reason.

EMPEROR. The jealousies of nations——

CULTURE. All are guilty there. Jealousy, not love of money, is the root of all evil. That was a misprint. Yet I know of nothing those others want that is yours to give, save Peace. What do you want of them? Bites out of each, and when they refuse to be dismembered you cry "The blood be on their head, they force me into war."

EMPEROR. Germany must expand. That is her divine mission. I have it from on high.

CULTURE. Your system of espionage is known to be tolerably complete.

EMPEROR. All Germany is with me. I hold in leash the mightiest machine for war the world has forged.

CULTURE. I have seen your legions, and all are with you. Never was a lord more trusted. O Emperor, does that not make you pause?

EMPEROR. France invades little Belgium.

CULTURE. Chivalrous France! Never. Emperor, I leave you. One last word to you at the parting of the ways. France, Russia, Britain, these are great opponents, but it is not they will bring the pillars of Germany down. Beware of Belgium!

(*She goes. He is left in two minds; he crosses to sign, flings down pen, strikes bell.* CHANCELLOR *and* OFFICER *reappear.*)

CHANCELLOR. Your Imperial Majesty has signed?

EMPEROR. Thus! (*He tears the paper.*)

OFFICER. Sire!

EMPEROR. Say this to Russia, France, and Britain in my Imperial name: So long as they keep within their borders, I remain in mine.

OFFICER. But, sire——

EMPEROR. You know as I do, that is all they ask for.

CHANCELLOR. You were the friend of Austria!

EMPEROR. I'll prove it. Tell her from me

that Serbia has yielded on every point which doth become a nation, and that Austria may accept her terms.

CHANCELLOR. Nay, sire——

EMPEROR. And so there will be no war.

OFFICER. Sire, we beg——

EMPEROR. These are my commands.

(*They have to go, chagrined but deferential.*)

EMPEROR. The decision lay with me, and I said, "There shall be peace"; that be my zenith!

(*He goes back to the chair; he sleeps peacefully; in the distance a bell tolls the Angelus, and suddenly this is broken by one boom of a great gun, which reverberates and should be startling. The Spirit of Culture returns, now with a wound in her breast. She surveys him sadly.*)

CULTURE. Sleep on, unhappy King. (*He grows restless.*) Nay, better to wake, if even your dreams appal you.

(*He wakes, and for a moment he scarcely understands that he has been dreaming. The realisation is tragic to him.*)

EMPEROR. You! You have come here to mock me.

CULTURE. Oh, no.

EMPEROR. I dreamt there was no war. In my dream they came to me and I forbade the war. I saw the Fatherland smiling and prosperous, as it was before the war.

CULTURE. It was you who made the war, O Emperor!

EMPEROR. Belgium?

CULTURE. There is no Belgium now, but over what was Belgium there rests a soft light as of a halo, and through it is a flaming sword.

EMPEROR. I dreamt I had kept my plighted word to Belgium.

CULTURE. It was you, O Emperor, who broke your plighted word and laid waste the land. In the lust for victory you violated even the Laws of War which men contrive so that when the sword is sheathed they may dare again face their Maker. Your way to Him is lighted now by smouldering spires and ashes that were once fair academic groves of mine. And you shall seek Him over roads cobbled with the moans of innocents.

EMPEROR. In my dream I thought England was grown degenerate and would not fight.

CULTURE. She fought you where Crecy was and Agincourt and Waterloo, with all their dead to help her. The dead became quick in their ancient graves, stirred by the tread of the island feet, and they cried out: "How is England doing?" The living answered the dead upon their bugles with the "All's well." England, O Emperor, was grown degenerate, but you have made her great again.

EMPEROR. France, Russia?

CULTURE. They are here, around your walls.

EMPEROR. My people?

CULTURE. I see none marching, but men whose feet make no sound. Shades of your soldiers, who pass on and on in never-ending lines.

EMPEROR. Do they curse me?

CULTURE. None. They all salute you as they pass. They have done your bidding.

EMPEROR. The women curse me?

CULTURE. Not even the women. They, too, salute you. You were their father and could do no wrong.

EMPEROR. And you?

CULTURE. I have come with this gaping wound in my breast, to bid you farewell.

EMPEROR. God cannot let my Germany be utterly destroyed.

CULTURE. If God is with the Allies, Germany will not be destroyed. Farewell.

> (*She is going. She lifts a pistol from the table and puts it in his hand. She goes with shining eyes. The penny dip burns low. The great Emperor is lost in its shadows.*)